Collins

Get that Job

IN **7** SIMPLE STEPS

Collins

HarperCollins Publishers
77-85 Fulham Palace Road
Hammersmith
London W6 8JB

First edition 2014

10 9 8 7 6 5 4 3 2 1

© HarperCollins Publishers 2014

ISBN 978-0-00-750716-0

Collins® is a registered trademark of HarperCollins Publishers Limited

www.collins.co.uk

A catalogue record for this book is available from the British Library

Typeset in India by Aptara

Printed and bound in Great Britain by Clays Ltd, St Ives plc

The Publisher and author wish to thank the following rights holders for the use of copyright material: Step 2: extract from *The Nature of Human Values* by Milton Rokeach, adapted with the permission of the Simon & Schuster Publishing Group from The Free Press Edition, copyright © 1973 by The Free Press. Copyright © renewed 2001 by Sandra Ball Rokeach. All rights reserved; Step 3: extracts from the Strengthscope® technical manual and report, reproduced by permission of Strengths Partnership and Dr Paul Brewerton. Every effort has been made to contact the holders of copyright material, but if any have been inadvertently overlooked, the Publisher will be pleased to make the necessary arrangements at the first opportunity.

Illustrations by Scott Garrett

MIX
Paper from
responsible sources
FSC™ C007454

Find out more about HarperCollins and the environment at
www.harpercollins.co.uk/green

Contents

About the author

Peter Storr is a Chartered Occupational Psychologist with many years' experience in helping people to identify their key strengths and in interviewing and assessing candidates at organisations such as the BBC and King's College London. He has applied many of the principles outlined in this book to himself and he now runs his own business. He is also the author of *The Psychological Manager*, which was shortlisted for the Chartered Management Institute/British Library *Management Book of the Year* award in 2013, and he writes a regular blog on www.thepsychologicalmanager.com.

Step 1

PLAN YOUR HUNT AND KEEP IT MOVING

*"Knowing that we are responsible – "responseable" –
is fundamental to our effectiveness and to every
other habit of effectiveness.* — Stephen R. Covey:
The 7 Habits of Highly Effective People

Five ways to succeed

- ■ Recognise that you are responsible for your own career.

- ■ Make a 'Get that job' plan and regularly review it.

- ■ Create an 'elevator pitch' and practise it.

- ■ Create a network and keep in touch with your contacts.

- ■ Know what helps you stay motivated when things get tough.

Five ways to fail

- ■ Assume that a dream job is going to fall into your lap.

- ■ Fire off a stream of random applications and hope for the best.

- ■ Make the assumption that people will know what you want.

- ■ Try to do it all yourself without support.

- ■ Give up after a couple of attempts.

The changing job market

How it used to be ...

Let me start with a personal example. I left school in 1980 and got a job in a bank. I didn't mean to really; it just happened. I remember having a chat with the school careers officer who suggested banking was a good idea, but to be honest I don't think I gave it any more thought than that. What seemed to be important is that I got a job – any job – and that was that. I also seem to remember (it has got lost in the mists of time, rather) the job interview going something like this:

Them: Why do you want this job?

Me: Well, it sounded interesting and I'm good with numbers, I think.

Them: Congratulations! You're in. You'll retire when you're 65.

I'm sure it wasn't really like that, but it wasn't far off. I got an interview at the first time of trying, too, and without really trying at all. It doesn't work like that now, and it could be argued that it shouldn't: I got a job that I wasn't really interested in, wasn't very good at and it was a rather unfulfilling period of my life – and they got someone who was average at best.

How it is now

Wind forward 30 years and things couldn't be more different. There is no such thing as failsafe job security, it's rare to get a job at the first time of trying and even rarer to be offered a job if you haven't done your homework. Perhaps the major change though is in who is responsible for our career path. In my case, I was made to feel like I was a passive recipient of my future, with no control or accountability; as long as I went through the motions, I would fulfil the destiny presented to me.

Nowadays, it's us, the jobseekers, more than ever, who are responsible. We've had to replace security in our employers with security in our employability; in other words, it's up to us to build the transferable knowledge, skills and abilities to take from one employer to another, in a kind of 'portfolio'. We are now in charge of our careers, which is both empowering and a little scary.

What does this mean for getting that job?

By now it will be clear that, today, merely sending off a few CVs to a few organisations you like the sound of and hoping for the best just doesn't cut the mustard. You need to be proactive, to have a plan or a strategy for job hunting because job hunting is best thought of as a process; a sequence of steps that should be followed to maximise your chances of success. The simple truth is that employers expect prospective employees to show initiative and take charge of their own destinies. Taking the initiative is not about being aggressive, arrogant or overbearing. It's about deciding to make things happen and then creating a plan to make them more likely to.

While it's not always easy, and at times may be frustrating and disheartening, many people find it rather satisfying to make a plan and monitor its progress, analysing the results and learning from what worked and what didn't. If you can share your plans, ideas, successes and failures with others who are in the same position as you, then that extra support and mutual encourage-ment can be invaluable. You also need to periodically review your plans and give them occasional reality checks. There is a saying: 'The first sign of madness is to keep on doing the same things and expecting different results.' If something seems not to be working, change it!

Your 'Getting that job' plan

So, what might your 'Getting that job' plan look like? The precise nature and components of your plan depend on the type of job you're looking for. Graduate and managerial job selection processes often include assessments such as a presentation, role-play exercises or exercises that assess planning and organisational abilities. Other jobs may have manual dexterity tests or verbal/numerical reasoning tests or personality assessments, but essentially they are all just ways of ensuring that *you* fit the job and that the job fits you.

Most plans tend to cover the following areas:

■ **Stage 1: Doing the groundwork**
Researching, networking, creating a plan, deciding what you want, clarifying your skills and strengths (see Steps 1, 2 and 3 of this book)

■ **Stage 2: Getting ready to apply**
Creating a CV template, building a portfolio of evidence of competencies (see Step 4)

■ **Stage 3: Preparing for interviewing and other assessments**
Presenting yourself, preparing for typical interview questions and understanding what assessments are likely to be used (see Steps 5 and 6)

■ **Stage 4: Reviewing progress and keeping up to date**
Reviewing your job search process: what went well, what you could do differently next time, what development is needed

By following a process like this, you'll put yourself in the best possible position to get that job.

Networking in your job search

It should now be clear that to be successful in job hunting, as in anything, it's best to seize the initiative, to take control of the job hunting process – and to treat it like a process. Later steps in this book will take this a stage further, when we look at what you want to achieve and why you are the ideal candidate for specific jobs. Identifying the actions required during Step 1 will be easier if you're aware of how you might find a job to apply for in the first place.

Of course, you may hear about a job through a relative, friend or someone you know. There's nothing wrong with this – far from it – and your chances of this happening are greatly increased if you widen your circle of contacts. Most of us do this naturally and spontaneously, but we can (and should) also be more targeted and strategic about it. This is called 'networking'. Think about your reactions to that word. As soon as we make it sound formal, a 'thing' we should be doing, it suddenly becomes scary. It's worth practising and persevering though; a great many people become aware of a potential opportunity through someone they know.

Remember that this is not about getting an unfair advantage over others or being neatly slotted into a vacancy. When we have a good network we simply hear about more opportunities than we would otherwise – and there are more people potentially looking out for us.

Why it works

So, networking is, to put it simply, building our networks. Everybody is at the centre of their own network, a bit like a spider is in the middle of its web, and the further you can spin your web, the more chances you will have of hearing of opportunities that might have otherwise passed you by.

The principle is exactly the same as in selling: a 'warm' lead is far more likely to result in success than a 'cold' call. The fact that there's an initial contact or relationship, no matter how small, is what seems to make the difference between a sale and no sale – and when you're job hunting, you are in effect selling yourself. If we are recommended by someone else, that has a very powerful impact indeed. It's probably the best possible strategy you can have for standing out from the crowd.

Don't forget, however, that your network doesn't end simply with the name on the list. Each name in your network will have their own network, so by implication you are in their network too, if at a stage removed. There are many instances of people hearing about a job through a contact of a contact, so the more people who know who you are, what you're good at and what you're looking for, the better your chances.

The good news is that networking is simple. Once you've made a list of everyone you know, it's simply a matter of contacting them. The trick is to be strategic, and to have a plan. Don't just send out a generic email to everyone on your list and hope for the best. Think about how you would feel if your friends did that. It's far better to target your communication – to tailor the message to the recipient. Let's look at this in more detail.

Building your network

The starting point for creating your network is simple, as we said earlier: to list everyone you know. Set yourself a target. If you can get to between 150 and 200 people in your first draft, then you're well on your way! Don't worry if it feels like a bit of a 'stretch' to include some of the names in your network; you can always prune it later. You may find the following list helpful to get you started:

- Family

- Friends

- Friends of friends

- People you have worked with in the past

- People you work with now

- People your partner knows

- Neighbours

- People you know from your hobbies or sporting activities

- Customers you have had a good experience with

- People you know through voluntary work

- People who have supplied services to you or your workplace

- Old school or university friends

Making contact

When you've made your list, the next stage is to contact each person to let them know that you're looking for the next opportunity to further your career. Some people find it helpful to write out a script in advance of a telephone call; in any event, whatever means of communication you choose, be clear about the following:

■ How you come to be contacting this person; in other words, how you got their name (unless this is obvious).

■ A very brief summary of why and how this person may be able to help you. Note, asking them directly for a job is not a good idea; it's too blunt and may make them feel they have been put on the spot. It's far better to ask if they know of one, or to ask for any advice they can give as to how to find one, or if they know of someone else who could help.

■ Your current situation and what, precisely, you're looking for.

It's important to bear in mind that if they have no advice to give or haven't heard of a specific opportunity, this is far from a wasted effort! By contacting them, you have planted a seed that may come to fruition many months down the line, and you have also reminded them of who you are, which makes it more likely that they'll think of you should a suitable opportunity arise.

Using social media

Many people find using some form of social media helpful in developing and maintaining contacts and networks and becoming alert to job opportunities. In fact, nowadays it's fair to say that it's become essential. Like any system, however, it's only as good as the data you put into it and the particular methods or sites that you use. And remember – it's only a tool and is only part of the process. Many people fall into the trap of thinking that having a LinkedIn® page (a great idea), and connecting with people on it, is the same thing as networking. Having a presence on sites such as LinkedIn® has several benefits:

- They help you keep track of your contacts and of their contact details.

- They help you keep up to date with what your contacts are doing.

- They enable you to post a brief summary of your work experience, key skills and attributes all in one place, and in a place that you can easily keep up to date.

- You can post messages about what you're doing and what you're looking for.

- You can receive and read messages from others.

- It doesn't cost anything!

You can use social media to your advantage in other ways, too. If you have a Twitter or Facebook account, follow or connect with the organisations you're either applying to join or would be interested in joining; you'll get a feel for the organisation's style and key issues and concerns, and it's a way of demonstrating enthusiasm, creative thinking and a degree of understanding of how the digital world works. It may be of benefit to start your own blog – maybe about your job search itself. Bloggers are the internet's thought leaders, and you can link your blog to your profiles on LinkedIn® and Facebook. This would then, for example, go out to your connections on the weekly update email. If you search or connect with companies you're interested in, you can look for employees of that company who are connected to those in your own network. You could then ask your connections for a connect request with those people you have identified.

A couple of other tips:

■ Regularly update your status to inform your connections across all social media of any relevant activities, such as training, achievements, articles you've read, book reviews. It will help them remain aware of your job search and interests.

■ Similarly, post regular updates on your progress on all your social media sites; you may want to update your contacts on what you're looking for, interviews you've attended, people you've met.

A word of warning, however: be very careful about what you post on social networking sites. There have been cases where individuals have had to resign over inappropriate postings on social media sites. Many employers and recruiters check the Facebook and Twitter accounts of job applicants. You can't go far wrong if you never post anything publicly on any form of social media that you wouldn't want a prospective employer (or interviewer) to see. This applies to activities you write about, pictures that you may not want the wider public to see, and also the language you use. You can set up Facebook so it informs you of picture tags to enable you to view them before they're published. You can't stop them being 'out there' but you can stop them being identified with you. Likewise, be careful about what you post on anyone else's Facebook page or website too – you will no longer have control of it and you may even need them to delete it for you.

If you are worried about anything that's already in the public domain, some websites suggest moving those items off that profile and setting up another profile (a social media alias using a different name) so that you end up having both a professional and personal online profile. The first profile, with your correct name, then becomes your professional profile with content that you are happy to share with prospective employers.

You can type your name into any of the major search engines to find anything you may have forgotten about – and remember, if you can do this, so can a prospective employer, and more of them are starting to do so.

Networking in the field

Sometimes we get the opportunity to attend a function (such as a seminar or conference) where networking is one of the main reasons to go – or at least, a very useful side issue! The trick is to have a well-practised script to fall back on to help you get your key message across and to reduce the fear of running out of small talk.

- Before you attend the function, prepare. If you had only 20 or so seconds between floors in an elevator to get the essence of 'you' across to a stranger, what would you say? This is the 'elevator pitch'.

- Remember that people love to talk about themselves, so first ask what they do and why they're there, what they have enjoyed and what they're intending to see, and then move on to talking about yourself and what you're looking for.

17

Sounding pro

Usually, once a networking conversation has started, it looks after itself – it's the getting going that feels like the most difficult part. Remember these basic rules:

- Have an elevator pitch rehearsed.
- Even if you don't feel like it, smile!
- Introduce yourself confidently, then ask about the other person.
- Ask questions and make comments about the nature of their job and their organisation, if you can.
- Turn the topic of attention to you at an appropriate point.
- When the conversation reaches a natural close, end it politely and smile again! If it's appropriate, give your contact details and ask them to get in touch if they hear of a suitable opportunity. Use your judgement. Did the other person seem to enjoy the conversation? Were they interested in what you had to say?

Introducing yourself	*Hi. I'm Jon. Nice to meet you. …*
Using questions and comments to show interest in the other person	*What have you enjoyed so far? / What were you hoping to get out of this event? / What do you do? / Where do you work? / That sounds like a really creative place to work.*
Turning the topic of conversation to you	*That sounds very interesting. I'm currently looking for my next opportunity. I'm here because I'm looking for a sales role in the technology industry.*
Ending the conversation	*It's been very nice to meet you. / I've enjoyed meeting you very much.*

For more information on networking, see *Successful Networking in 7 Simple Steps*, published by HarperCollins.

Where else to find jobs

It's fair to say that a large number of people get jobs – or at least hear about them – through their networks. Increasing the size and scope of yours will help you hear about those opportunities as they arise. Of course, you can't only rely on your network – both real and virtual – to find job opportunities, even though it is a good strategy. Try to widen your search, and improve your chances of success, by considering avenues such as these:

- **Newspaper adverts:** Look in all local papers, and even papers local to an area you would consider moving to.

- **Professional or specific industry magazines:** As well as scanning advertisements, it's a long shot to read an article and send a speculative letter, but you never know …

- **Libraries:** These are a greatly under-used resource by job hunters. Some libraries have job advertisement areas, and some larger ones hold job-seeking seminars.

- **Job centres:** One of the more obvious ways, but it's definitely worth registering your interest and checking regularly. Bear in mind that it's often jobs in the trades that are advertised in job centres.

Two of the most commonly used avenues are worth exploring in a bit more depth. Many people register with recruitment agencies, either specialist sector-specific ones or more generalist ones, and increasingly, job hunters are turning to internet job search sites to find opportunities.

Recruitment agencies

Some recruitment agencies are fabulous and are staffed by professionals who really want to help you find a job. And some are less good. But they are a useful resource for finding many types of job, and some organisations only advertise through specific agencies. As long as you understand that, like estate agents, they're working primarily for their client, not you, and that they usually have an incredibly heavy workload so will tend to keep communication to a minimum, then there's no harm in allowing them to help you. Follow these tips for dealing effectively with recruitment agencies:

- Identify the most relevant recruitment agencies for the type of work or sector you're interested in.

- Be prepared to ask them questions about how the process works: what they require of you and what you can expect of them; how and when communication should be conducted and any advice they can give you.

- Be clear about what you want – and only go for jobs you would be prepared to accept. If the agency puts you forward for a job that you subsequently turn down without a good reason, they'll be unlikely to consider you again.

- Always be honest: your reputation as someone who is straightforward to deal with is worth its weight in gold.

- Make sure you come across to them and to any company you are referred to in a way that makes you look good: never be late; always be polite; present yourself appropriately.

Internet job search sites

Registering with internet job search sites has become an incredibly popular method of looking for work for one simple reason: everything is there in one place, to be accessed whenever and wherever you like. Employers can advertise vacancies and search through pre-uploaded CVs to see if there are any initial matches. Job hunters can get career advice through articles and online tutorials or webinars. They can also get advice on how to build an effective CV (although this advice may be tailored to the format they want for CVs to be uploaded to their particular site). And, of course, you can search for job vacancies – by job type or title, salary, location and specific organisation. You can also register to get immediate notification of vacancies sent directly to your phone or email address.

Some have links to related career services elsewhere, such as the Chartered Institute for Personnel and Development (CIPD) and the Open University, where you can get advice on flexible learning and development or enhancing and building on your qualifications. Others have links to – or even arrange themselves – career roadshows that travel around the country giving advice and putting job seekers and local employers together. These usually include masterclasses in CV writing and interview techniques. There are many of these internet job search sites, but some of the most popular are:

- Monster (www.monster.co.uk)
- Reed (www.reed.co.uk)
- TotalJobs (www.totaljobs.com)
- Fish4Jobs (www.fish4.co.uk)

Finally, do remember to keep everything you have uploaded to these sites up to date.

Keeping motivated

Job hunting does require a certain amount of resilience, and keeping motivated when you've been rejected a few times can be difficult. It's easy to take to heart stories you hear of people sending 100 job applications a day without success, but let's put this into perspective. It's far more efficient to channel your efforts, energy and motivation into a meaningful, targeted plan rather than a generic scattergun approach, and applying in this way is far more likely to keep your motivation higher. Creating a plan, sticking to it and reviewing regularly what's working is going to keep your resilience levels up and your drive to achieve your end goal more focused.

Some people find keeping a diary is helpful for monitoring progress, but most at least find keeping some sort of written record of actions and results achieved useful. Ensure you make a note of progress achieved during the week – even if you haven't got a firm end result you can usually identify steps you've made towards your end goal. Don't underestimate the importance of celebrating even small wins and successes on your job hunting journey; it releases feel-good chemicals similar to the endorphins experienced by long-distance runners!

If you're one of those individuals motivated by variety (see Step 2), then varying your approach during the week may keep your energy levels up. Pursuing a variety of avenues will not only increase your chances of success, but will have the knock-on effect of keeping your interest levels up too. It may take months to find a job that you really want (rather less if you're prepared to take the view that being in any job is a good springboard to finding one you really want), so think about what will keep you going; don't be one of the many people who give up after a couple of months. Your dedication to the process and your determination to succeed are likely to impress any subsequent interviewer – and would be a good example if asked the question: 'When have you had to demonstrate resilience in achieving a goal?'

Key take-aways

Think about the things you will take away from Step 1 and how you will implement them.

Topic	Take-away	Implementation
Understanding what the job market is like now and how this affects your job search	• Recognise that I am responsible for my own job search. • Security is in my employability, not my employer.	• Take charge of my career choices. • Be proactive in my job search. • Think of skills being transferable and start building my portfolio.
Creating a plan to 'Get that job'		
How to use networking to help your job search		
Using social media to help your job search		
Where to find jobs		
Keeping motivated		

Step 2

UNDERSTAND WHAT YOU WANT

'There is no such thing as a career path. There is only crazy paving and you have to lay it yourself.'
— Sir Dominic Cadbury, former chairman of Cadbury, the chocolate manufacturer

Five ways to succeed

- Think about where you would like to get to in the longer term.

- Identify what interests you and how this may relate to jobs.

- Determine your core values and what this means.

- Clarify what would really motivate you at work.

- Remember that work does not have to fulfil all your needs.

Five ways to fail

- Never spend time thinking about your future.

- Assume that work is what you do, not who you are.

- Wait for that perfect job that is the answer to everything.

- Make work and getting a job just about the money.

- Don't believe that work can be enjoyable.

Identifying your interests, values and motivation

There is an ancient Chinese saying: 'A thousand mile journey begins with a single step.' In Step 1 we looked at how your job hunting journey starts with understanding the world of work and at the importance of taking control of the job hunting process so you can meet it head on. The next stage is to work out what you want by looking at your interests and values and what motivates you. This is based on a very simple premise: we do best what we most enjoy. If we enjoy something, we try harder and are more motivated, which leads to higher performance. And higher performance leads to more possibilities – and more probability – of promotion. All of this leads to expanding our potential avenues for work and futures we never even dreamed of. It all starts with being good at whatever you do – whatever it is you are doing – because you never know where it might lead you.

Performing well and keeping motivation up are not always easy, especially if you're currently doing a job which you don't particularly enjoy or you feel is beneath you. Remember that resilience is a key – and learnable – skill; one of the most transferable!

A job or a career?

So, at this stage in your job search, what is it that you want? Is it a job or a career? What is the difference? Indeed, is there a difference any more?

Back in the distant past when I applied for that first banking role, there most definitely was a difference. A job was something you did that did not necessarily lead to anything else apart from a salary and work experience. A career was meant to be for life, and had qualifications and a career path and there was usually just one way of getting there: steady progression up the chain of command.

It would be ridiculous to say that the career is dead, but it is nowhere near as rigid a concept as 30 years ago. It was a very limiting concept – you 'were' a banker or an accountant or a member of the Armed Forces, and once you were, that's what you stayed. Being asked at 18: 'What do you want to do for the rest of your working life?' sounds like nonsense, but many people still feel forced into coming up with something.

If we take the idea of the portfolio of transferable skills we mentioned in Step 1, we increase our options and create our own future, mixing and matching a varied sequence of inter-linked careers. Every job or mini-career has a set of transferable skills and experiences which can lead to a multitude of futures – futures that we construct ourselves. In the end, the job or career question becomes redundant.

Identifying your interests

We said earlier that we tend to be good at what we enjoy. The same is true of what interests us. What interests us and what we're good at aren't quite the same, however: we can be good at 'things' but are interested in an idea or a particular discipline or sector. For example, you may be fascinated by the world of accounting and finance; this may relate to being good with numbers, but it's not necessarily the same thing.

If you are fortunate enough to have a clear interest or desire to work in a particular area, then you are indeed very lucky. You may have to be flexible and creative in how you break into that sector if you're not in it already, but knowing that you want to get there is a great start. It makes your targeting of that sector more simple and elegant, and when we come to Step 3 (Know your skills and strengths) you will be able to ensure they reflect the sector you have aspirations to join or progress in. We'll mention this again later, but a great principle to live by is: 'Begin with the end in mind' – work out what you want to achieve and work backwards.

I mentioned at the start of this book that I began my professional working life as a bank clerk. I hadn't been particularly happy in this role for a couple of years, but – sensibly, some might argue – I didn't feel that I could leave until I knew what I wanted to leave *to*. It took a while for me to go from 'banking isn't it' to 'studying psychology *is*'. Once I had a good idea of where I wanted to go, it was far easier to take the plunge!

Many of us, however, are not clear about what we ultimately want. It's important not to get demoralised by this. Not many people wake up when they're 15 and say to themselves: 'I want to be a doctor' and then follow through on the ten-year plan to get there. Those that do are usually successful (as the 'Begin with the end in mind' principle would suggest), but it doesn't happen for most of us.

If you have clear interests career-wise, then so much the better. If not, what then? Well, to start with, the links between our interests and the world of work are not always obvious – and indeed, we may have separated them in our head: '*This is what I'm interested in, and this is what I will do for a living …*'. It's a useful exercise to occasionally question the assumptions we have allowed ourselves to believe.

29

You may think that it's obvious to you what your interests are. But it's worth going through this exercise because many of us don't make the link between our interests and the world of work. They don't have to be the same (you may have an interest in the natural world but don't necessarily want a career in it), but it may prompt some ideas. And if you can work in an area where you have a personal interest, it won't feel as much like work.

Ask yourself these questions and write the answers down:

- What do you find yourself drawn to when you read a newspaper?

- What non-fiction books do you read for fun?

- What do your friends think you are particularly knowledgeable about?

- What particularly interested you at school?

- What are your main hobbies?

- What is it about these hobbies that particularly interests you?

- What would you say are your key interests?

- If you were forced to give a presentation on any subject, what would it be?

- What jobs or careers might link to these areas of interest?

- Does anyone in the network you identified in Step 1 have links with these areas?

- Who else do you know who has this interest? What are their ideas?

Determining your values

As well as working out what interests us, determining our values can also help us to identify what we want from our work. Values are our core beliefs about what is right and wrong and what is important to us. The culture we were brought up in, the way we were parented, our religion and our experiences as children and as adults all have an impact on our values. They can be treated as a route map: an inner voice or guide – or sometimes our conscience – and ultimately lead us to determining our behaviours and attitudes.

When we act against these values, we get a 'pricking' of our conscience. Psychologists call this 'cognitive dissonance'. It's an unpleasant feeling and it's unpleasant for a reason: it's there in order to prompt us to change either the belief/attitude or the behaviour, to make the tension go away. If you were vegetarian and got a job in a butcher's shop, for example, the tension between your values and your behaviour would make it harder to perform well because you wouldn't enjoy it. It's always worth listening to this tension – this inner voice – because when we behave in accordance with our values, we become more fulfilled by what we're doing.

Rokeach's list of personal values

A well-known model of values was developed in the 1970s by Milton Rokeach, a Polish-American social psychologist. He suggested that the following values have an impact on our behaviour and we will each have our particular favourites – the ones that guide us the most. Read the following list and choose the five that say the most about how you prefer to behave in order to achieve what you want in life.

Value	
Cheerfulness	
Ambition	
Love	
Cleanliness	
Self-control	
Capability	
Courage	
Politeness	
Honesty	
Imagination	
Independence	
Intellect	
Broad-mindedness	
Logic	
Obedience	
Helpfulness	
Responsibility	
Forgiveness	

If you can, think about the order of importance for you of your five values. How do they help you when things get tough? What do they say about how you can conduct your job search? And how do they help you determine or have an influence on the line of work you are most suited to?

Determining what motivates you

Motivation has been studied for close to 100 years. Initially, the research seemed to be saying that people are primarily motivated by money; if we want people to work harder, we pay them more. If we had enough money, we wouldn't work.

We now know that this is far too simplistic. Of course, money can be a motivator to us, and when you are out of work it may be a key driver towards getting employment. This, of course, is entirely natural and understandable. But it's important to realise that once we are in work, and our basic survival needs are met, then for most of us money ceases to be the powerful motivator it was to start with.

There are other things that cause us to be satisfied with work apart from a good salary: like-minded colleagues or a nice corner office, for example. However, research over the last 50 years or so has tended to concentrate on money as being the one thing. So, if money and the other trappings of employment are limited as to the effect they have on our motivation, what does have a motivational effect? This is an important question for one very good reason: we are all different.

What makes us different?

We differ from each other in many ways. Psychologists have tended to separate the ways we differ at a psychological level into four main categories which are largely distinct from each other.

■ We differ in terms of our intellect – how clever we are. This is often measured by IQ tests, but for our purposes it's primarily concerned with our ability to reason logically.

■ We also differ in terms of our personality. There are many ways in which personality can vary, and many theories to describe these differences, such as whether we have a preference for extroversion or introversion, for example.

■ We differ in the amount of knowledge, skills and abilities we have; not our intellect exactly, but more our experience and (ideally) transferable skills.

■ Finally, we differ in terms of our motivation, both in terms of how motivated we are in general, and in what motivates us – our key motivational drivers. These change as we go through life but there is often an essence that stays with us.

The reason why this last one, motivation, is so important is that, depending on the job itself, it probably has the biggest influence of all these differences on how well we do something.

Your motivational drivers

I've often said, as a manager of people: 'Give me a team that is highly motivated over a team that is highly skilled any day.' I mean it, too. Motivated people learn fast, are proactive and can be trusted to do their best. The trick as a manager is to know the individual motivations of your staff. For the job hunter, knowing your key motivational drivers can help you target your job search and perform to the best of your ability once you are in a job.

Merely asking yourself: 'What motivates me?' may not help you, however. Most of us don't know – or at least, haven't given it any structured thought. The question is too abstract without giving it a framework, and this is where modern motivation questionnaires come in; they get at these answers through the back door. You don't need to use the questionnaire approach, of course (you have to be qualified to be able to use some of them, in any event), but these questionnaires have distilled the research into a framework of motivating factors that you can choose from.

One such questionnaire and supporting motivation framework has been developed by Dr Paul Brewerton. The model he has proposed assesses 11 factors that can either be motivators or demotivators (by their absence) at work. Knowing what your key ones tend to be (and which ones are not particularly important to you) can help you decide on a particular type of work or a preferred organisational culture.

These 11 factors are:

- **Affiliation:** a desire to work closely with other people, getting to know them and being at the centre of social events

- **Recognition:** a desire for acknowledgement for your efforts and receiving positive feedback from others

- **Caring:** a desire to nurture others in the work role and being seen as a shoulder to cry on by others

- **Independence:** a desire to work autonomously without the heavy involvement of superiors; valuing personal freedom

- **Development:** a desire for ongoing personal and professional development through training, coaching and other learning opportunities

- **Responsibility:** a desire to take positions of responsibility and influence over others; valuing the status associated with more senior positions

- **Achievement:** a desire to set and achieve stretching goals; being recognised for achieving them

- **Variety:** a desire to do original, creative, interesting work; valuing work environments which encourage innovation

- **Material:** a desire to make money and achieve a good remunerative package

- **Security:** a desire to work in a secure and stable role and organisation; more likely than most to believe in the 'job for life' model

- **Environment:** a desire to be happy and comfortable in the physical working environment

As with the *interests* exercise earlier in this step, pick the ones that most appeal to you; the ones that your ideal job would satisfy. No job is perfect, and no job can satisfy all of your key motivational drivers (and certainly not at the same time), but being aware of what they are may help to narrow down your choices of occupations and organisations. Remember that you work at your best and are at your most fulfilled when your interests, values and motivations are being satisfied as much as possible.

Motivations change as we go through our working life and gain in experience and knowledge of ourselves. Keeping up to date with what's motivating us can ensure we are constantly assessing our job and our career, and enable us to make rational career choices.

Maintaining balance: filling the doughnut

It's important, in the midst of all this self-reflection, to keep a balanced perspective. As previously mentioned, no one job can satisfy everything we want or address all aspects of our interests and motivations. We have lives outside of work which can also address some of our needs.

Charles Handy, a best-selling author and business consultant, has written extensively of the doughnut principle, including in his book *The Empty Raincoat: Making Sense of the Future.* Imagine a doughnut (the sort with a hole in the middle, as opposed to one filled with jam), but then reverse it so it is the hole that has the substance. The doughnut of empty space around it, with its invisible boundary, represents the 'what could be' and the core (what used to be the hole) represents our core duties. The space beyond is our chance to make a difference in the job – or express elements of our interests, values and motivations outside of it. Handy goes a step further; he suggests that it's our ultimate responsibility in life to fulfil this potential. It's not limitless as there is a boundary, but most of us tend to lose our sense of perspective and focus only on the core of our personal doughnut.

An example may help. You may see a job in a software design company that you want to apply for. It has many of the attributes that make it motivating to you; it taps into your desire for independence, variety and responsibility. It's also related to an area of interest which you enjoy reading about and keeping up to date with – you spend a lot of your time in computer shops and you design apps in your spare time. The organisation itself seems to identify with the sorts of values of creativity and innovation that you share. All these elements make up the core of the doughnut, and it's easy to limit your thinking to this core.

Handy invites us to identify this core – the 'what is' – and to use it to help us think about the 'what could be' – the empty space around it with its boundary. This might represent the complete us: our aspirations for the future; the expression of our values outside work; our family life; the hobbies and activities that make us well-rounded, balanced individuals with dreams for the future.

The lesson is that the job itself – the current job we're doing or the one we're applying for – does not and should not provide everything we wish for, and we will be very dissatisfied if we expect it to. Your current job may not satisfy your need for affiliation – working closely with other people – for example, but many other aspects of your life outside the central core probably will.

You may need to think of the job you're in or applying for as a stepping stone to the next one. Some people, as we've mentioned, seem to have a fully formed career path and have identified the various steps it will take to get there, but most of us don't. It may help, however, to think one job ahead, at least.

Think about your responses to the following questions:

■ Would part-time work be a feasible option?

■ Would you consider a job-share arrangement?

■ Would you consider a combination of part-time and self-employed?

■ Could a maternity cover post or fixed term contract give you experience that may help you get the job you're really after?

■ Would you be prepared to undertake a series of fixed term contracts to gain experience?

■ How long would you be prepared to do this for?

■ If you could really begin with the end in mind, what is the minimum salary you would be prepared to accept now? What new avenues does that open up?

■ Can you find other ways of expressing your interests and motivations outside work as well as in it?

What often happens is that we unconsciously put blocks in place to stop us considering options such as these, and of course it's very easy to find reasons for not accepting any of them. We then automatically close these options down and don't give them any further consideration.

What's important, then, is that you at least go through the thought processes that may lead to you still discounting them – but from a position of awareness! For now, try to suspend your immediate judgement or initial feelings and look simply at the advantages and disadvantages of each.

It's easy to only focus on the next job and not view it in the context of your career journey. That doesn't mean you shouldn't strive to do your best in the one you have or are applying for – I've met many people who have not been engaged with their work because their sights are too firmly set on promotion, which paradoxically makes that promotion less likely to happen. But having an idea of the next challenge you'd like to take on can mean that you focus on the right things in this one. Remember the 'Begin with the end in mind' strapline, and, if necessary, take the long view. When you're in the depths of job hunting it can become all-encompassing and it's hard sometimes to raise your head up and think about the bigger picture – to think long term and not expect to get the whole doughnut in one fell swoop. In this way, you may open up new ways of thinking about what you want. You may then start asking yourself more searching questions that you may never have thought of before.

You may also like to try this exercise:

After reading Step 4 (Write a killer CV), write the CV you would like to have in, say, five years' time. After you've written it, imagine yourself there. Really take the time to reflect on it. Ask yourself the following questions:

■ Where are you working?

■ What are your main duties?

■ What were your key successes?

■ What does this say about your aspirations?

■ What are the differences between your CV then and now?

■ What can you start doing now to reduce that gap?

■ What have you learned from doing this exercise?

■ What is the first step you will take to make it happen?

Putting it all together

If the theme of Step 1 was proactivity – taking charge of your search for a job – then the theme of this Step 2 is 'Begin with the end in mind' – work out where it is you are headed so you can start making plans to get there.

And perhaps the most important message behind this step is that, to really succeed, to be good at what you do and progress along the pathway you have chosen, you need to enjoy it. There will always be elements of the job that are less interesting than others, but essentially we are at our best when we're doing something that draws us towards it because we want to do it.

It sounds obvious that we should align our work if we possibly can to our interests, values and motivations, but the simple truth is that many people do not go through that thought process. They end up, for very good reasons, in work that does not fulfil them and as a result drains energy, instead of generating it.

The final step in your journey of self-discovery is to look at your skills and strengths, and how these relate to what employers are looking for.

Key take-aways

Think about the things you will take away from Step 2 and how you will implement them.

Topic	Take-away	Implementation
Understanding the difference between a job and a career	• *We do best what we most enjoy.* • *We may need to take the longer view.* • *The more we identify where we want to go, the more likely it is to happen.*	• *Spend time thinking about my interests, values and key motivational drivers.* • *Think about my ultimate aspirations.* • *Identify some short-term measures which may get me there.*
Identifying your interests		
Determining your values		
Understanding what makes us different and how this impacts on your job search		
Identifying your motivational drivers		
Thinking beyond the core of the doughnut		
Learning from writing the CV you would like to have in five years		

Step 3

KNOW YOUR SKILLS AND STRENGTHS

'Argue for your limitations, and sure enough, they're yours.' — Richard Bach, author

Five ways to succeed

■ Think of yourself in marketing terms, i.e. as a brand.

■ As well as your values, identify your key strengths.

■ Use *competencies* when defining your skills.

■ Have a stock of examples of achievements from your past.

■ Write down your 'core essence' and remember it.

Five ways to fail

■ Think of brands as products, not people.

■ Assume that your skills will be obvious to anyone else.

■ Don't think about what competencies an employer wants.

■ Have no idea what your strengths are.

■ Assume that non-work experiences are irrelevant.

We can only control what we are aware of

Most theories of learning and development say pretty much the same thing: if we are unaware of something, it controls us. The opposite is therefore true – if we become aware of our strengths and weaknesses, we can make sure we either let them work for us or do something about them! The essence of this step follows this broad premise: if we know what our skills and strengths are, we can make sure we use them to our advantage. And that is very important when job hunting, because if you're sure about what your USPs are – your Unique Selling Points – you can make sure potential employers know what they are too.

In the previous step, we looked at your interests, values and motivations in order to lead you to consider what it is you want and why. This step is concerned with what you feel you're good at, what you feel your strengths are (which typically energise you when they're being displayed) and how these concepts, together with your skills, relate to what employers are looking for. We will end the step by refining and expanding on your elevator pitch, introduced in Step 1, which will then be the starting point for the next step – writing a killer CV.

The concept of 'Brand You'

At first glance, the heading may sound a bit strange. We're all used to seeing brand names for products and services all around us every day of our lives. We gradually attach meaning to those brands. We will associate some brands with quality, some with value, some with products and services we trust, and yet others with distaste! Think of five brands that you've been aware of in the past few days. Ask yourself these questions:

■ What thoughts and feelings do those brands conjure up?

■ What words would you use to describe them?

■ How do your thoughts and feelings about these brands influence what you buy?

Peculiar as it may seem, brands also apply to people. As with products and services, they act as a kind of shortcut so we don't have to build up a picture of them from scratch every time we think about them, see them or have to interact with them in some way. It's the same with people. For example, you may be thought of as someone who is reliable, trustworthy and consistent; you will have this label applied to you by those you know, so they don't ask themselves about your qualities every time they ask you to do something.

You have a brand. It's what people say about you when you're not in the room. It helps you to separate yourself from the competition when you're job hunting, to increase your visibility when you're looking for that promotion, and it also helps you to be clear about who you are and to ensure you're acting in ways that are true to who you are. It has built up over a long time, but it need not be hidden from you or beyond your control. It's a very useful exercise to think about how others might see you and how you wish to be seen. You can also shape it to make sure you're coming across in the way you intend and giving a clear message about who you are. You can think of your personal brand as comprising three core elements:

- **Your values:** we explored these in Step 2
- **Your skills and strengths:** we are exploring these in this step
- **Your essence:** your Unique Selling Points (USPs)

Identifying your values

Go back to the exercise outlined in Step 2 on page 32 (Rokeach's list of personal values). Remind yourself of the five values that you identified as saying the most about how you prefer to behave. Are they still the same or have you changed your mind in the intervening period? Is the order still the same? Remember that these act as your guide, your moral compass, and therefore affect how you behave.

Identifying your strengths

Strengths are different from values. Your strengths are those qualities that energise you when you're performing at your best, and when you appear full of energy. When you use your strengths at work, to help your job hunting, or merely to help you be clear about how to sell yourself when applying for jobs, you can be sure that you're coming across or performing at your best. When things are going well, playing to your strengths can help you to do even better.

A useful framework of 24 work-based strengths has been developed by the Strengths Partnership (www.strengthspartnership.com). These were chosen through research to depict the 24 strengths that have the biggest impact on work performance. A questionnaire is available through the Strengths Partnership, but we can use the following list. The first stage is to pick out your significant seven strengths – those that most energise you – by ticking them on the pages that follow.

Emotional strengths

Courage: you take on challenges and face risks by standing up for what you believe in	
Emotional control: you are aware of your emotional 'triggers' and how to control them	
Enthusiasm: you demonstrate passion and energy when communicating goals, beliefs, interests or ideas you feel strongly about	
Optimism: you remain positive and upbeat about the future and your ability to influence it	
Resilience: you deal effectively with setbacks and enjoy overcoming difficult challenges	
Self-confidence: you have a strong belief in yourself and your abilities to accomplish goals	

Relational strengths

Relationship building: you build networks of contacts and act as a hub between people	
Compassion: you demonstrate a genuine concern for the well-being and welfare of others	
Collaboration: you work cooperatively with others to overcome conflict and build towards a common goal	
Empathy: you identify with other people's situations and can see things from their perspective	
Persuasiveness: you are able to win agreement and support for a position or desired outcome	
Leading: you take responsibility for influencing and motivating others to contribute to success	
Developing others: you promote other people's learning and development to help them achieve their potential	

Thinking strengths

Creativity: you come up with new ideas and original solutions to move things forward	
Common sense: you make pragmatic judgements based on practical thinking and previous experience	
Critical thinking: you approach problems by breaking them down systematically and evaluating them objectively	
Strategic mindedness: you focus on the future and take a strategic perspective on issues and challenges	
Detail orientation: you pay attention to detail in order to produce high quality output, no matter what the pressures	

Execution strengths

Flexibility: you remain adaptable and flexible in the face of unfamiliar or changing situations	
Initiative: you take independent action to make things happen and achieve goals	
Results focus: you maintain a strong sense of focus on results, driving tasks and projects to completion	
Decisiveness: you make quick, confident and clear decisions, even when faced with limited information	
Efficiency: you take a well-ordered and methodical approach to tasks to achieve planned outcomes	
Self-improvement: you draw on a wide range of people and resources in the pursuit of self-development and learning	

Your significant seven strengths

It will be apparent that you probably use most of the 24 strengths from time to time, and that can make it difficult to choose between them. The idea is that we can hold around seven concepts or chunks of information in our head at any one time, so it's as good a number as any to start focusing our attention on the key strengths that energise you and describe you at your best.

Once you're happy with your significant seven, write them down and see if you spot any patterns amongst them. Do they tend to sit in one or two of the four categories? The Emotional and Relational strengths are more people-oriented, whereas the Thinking and Execution strengths are more task-oriented. Is there a theme here? How would your friends or colleagues describe you? Can you think of any examples that bring these strengths to light?

Your standout three strengths

Seven strengths is still a lot to hold in your head though. There is a saying that 'If you have more than three priorities, you have no priorities' – and it's difficult to concentrate fully on more than three of these strengths when faced with a real-life situation. Identifying the three standout strengths from your list of seven is useful to ensure that they are always at the back of your mind, so now choose the three that are most descriptive of you.

For each of these strengths, ask yourself the following questions:

My standout three strengths

1 _____

- ■ When have I demonstrated this strength?
- ■ How did it help achieve a successful outcome?
- ■ How did it help me meet a difficult challenge?

2 _____

- ■ When have I demonstrated this strength?
- ■ How did it help achieve a successful outcome?
- ■ How did it help me meet a difficult challenge?

3 _____

- ■ When have I demonstrated this strength?
- ■ How did it help achieve a successful outcome?
- ■ How did it help me meet a difficult challenge?

Identifying your skills

In Step 1 we introduced the concept of the portfolio career – one where we build up a collection of transferable skills and take them with us from job to job. The key word here is *transferable*; these skills are a very important part of what makes us employable.

If you're looking for your first job, you may have to be creative. You may, for example, need to point to the skills you developed while studying or doing voluntary work. These skills are not the same as qualifications, nor are they the same as personality traits or characteristics. Skills are things that you *can* do, not just what you *prefer* to do.

Competencies

Identifying your key skills is only half the story, however. Transferable skills are what employers are looking for, so you need to talk their language. Most employers use a system of putting 'families' of skills together into competencies – actual behaviours you can observe. Jobs are often condensed into between six and eight competencies and these are sometimes detailed in the job description.

Four common 'task' competencies

Planning and organising

Employers often want people who are able to plan their work and meet deadlines. Examples of behaviours looked for are:

■ Identifying the specific stages in a project

■ Being able to prioritise appropriately

■ Consistently delivering to agreed deadlines

■ Devising effective actions to work around problems

■ Setting up appropriate communication methods

Analytical thinking

Employers will often look for people who can analyse information and get to grips with the key issues of a problem. Examples of behaviours are:

■ Ability to simplify issues into component parts

■ Gathering all relevant information

■ Making links between different pieces of information

■ Identifying the root cause of problems

■ Anticipating potential barriers and/or risks

Decision making

Employers need people who can make clear, logical decisions which take into account all the relevant information. Examples are:

■ Being readily prepared to make decisions

■ Providing a suitable rationale for decisions

■ Considering the implications of decisions

■ Gathering information from all appropriate sources

■ Proposing appropriate solutions to problems

Adaptability

Employers look for people who are adaptable and flexible and open to change. Examples might include:

- Being willing to adapt to changing deadlines or fluid circumstances
- Embracing new technologies and new ways of working
- Showing openness to alternative ways of doing things
- Identifying when change is necessary and taking appropriate steps
- Responding positively to unexpected changes

Four common 'people' competencies

Teamworking

Employers always want people who can work constructively as part of a team. Example behaviours they may look for are:

- Working cooperatively with others to achieve team goals
- Playing an active not a passive role in the team
- Providing help and support to others when needed
- Constructively challenging others when required
- Encouraging team members to participate

Managing relationships

Employers also want people who can work constructively and positively with others in the organisation – or maybe customers or suppliers. Examples are:

- Seeking to understand others' needs, motivations and actions
- Demonstrating confidence when dealing with others
- Being tactful when dealing with others

- Responding sensitively to individual and/or cultural differences
- Managing others' expectations effectively

Communication

This is often one of the key skills looked for by organisations and it's hard to see where this wouldn't apply! Examples of behaviours looked for are:

- Adopting an appropriate style to suit the audience
- Sharing information openly with others
- Asking questions to clarify and obtain information
- Communicating in a clear, concise manner in both written and spoken forms
- Communicating with energy and enthusiasm

Influencing and persuading

Some jobs require an ability to win people over or change their minds – maybe to buy a product, for example. Employers may look for evidence of the following:

- Adapting style and/or argument to persuade people
- Showing awareness of differing perspectives
- Adopting a non-confrontational approach
- Using relevant information to support an argument
- Conveying the benefits of a suggested approach

The purpose of competencies

As we've seen, competencies are the shortcut that many organisations use to connect a job vacancy with a set of transferable skills. Each organisation will have its own set, varying with the level of the job being performed and sometimes designed specifically for that organisation. But most are fairly generic. What makes us employable for a specific job is a combination of our transferable skills and job- or sector-specific knowledge.

It may be up to you to pull out what competencies are being looked for when reading a job advert or reading the job description. However, most jobs will have elements of some of the competencies detailed on pages 55–57, so go through this list when trying to make sense of an application process that hasn't made it clear.

They are also useful as a way of determining your own key transferable skills to add into your 'Brand You' concept. The eight competencies should give you a flavour of the language used and the areas that these skills fall into. For simplicity, these competencies have been separated into task competencies and people competencies; in reality, a particular competency may include both people and task elements. Each competency usually has a heading, a description and a behavioural indicator – what the competency looks like in the flesh. We will revisit this idea when we look at the world of assessments in Step 6.

So what can you do with this information?

The aim of detailing these common competencies is to help you to realise that so many skills and attributes employers are looking for are fairly common and generic. They are the skills and experiences that have been identified as basic requirements for the job, and you will have to demonstrate that you can do them, or have done them. You'll notice, too, that they're not (or at least, should not be) vague descriptions that leave you guessing as to what the employer is looking for. They're written in behaviours – things that you can actually see or measure in some way. The whole point of competencies is that the skills requirements of the job in question are all made clear to all parties – this includes those people making the selection decisions within the organisation. This way, applicants for a job have an opportunity to either demonstrate the competencies at assessment or provide evidence and examples from the past of when they have demonstrated them.

Once you start thinking in this way, you can use competencies as a kind of shorthand for second-guessing what an employer is looking for if they haven't made it clear. For example, if you were applying for a job as a shop assistant, it's reasonably obvious that they would be looking for strong interpersonal skills, say, Communication, and Influencing and persuading. If the job was as a Personal Assistant, they would also want to include strong organising skills – Planning and organising, and Analytical thinking.

Thinking in this way and using this sort of language will help you in three ways:

■ It will allow you to think and talk about your transferable skills in the language that most employers use.

■ It will prepare you for interview by enabling you to go ready prepared with examples from the past of when you've been able to demonstrate the competencies they are looking for and tell them what the outcomes were.

■ It will prepare you for any assessments that may form part of the selection process. If assessments are used – even if it's merely a presentation as part of the interview – it's most likely that they'll be marking you against a set of competencies.

Thinking about your achievements

Some application forms and interviewers may ask questions about what you would do under certain circumstances, for example: 'What would you do if a customer shouted at you?' This is how interviews always used to be conducted and it's fair to say that many still are. However, nowadays questions about what you've done in the past are more common, for example: 'Tell me about a time when you've had to be extremely organised' or 'Tell me when you've had to give someone some tough feedback. What did you do, and what was the result?'

There is a very good reason for these questions: the best predictor of whether someone can demonstrate a skill, strength or competency in the future is whether they have done so in the past. If you talk about what you would do, not what you have done, it's easier to simply make it up!

Having a ready stock of examples of successes and achievements in your head during an interview is incredibly useful, as we shall go on to see in Step 5. Breaking these achievements down into competencies will help you and also ensure that you're talking the organisation's language.

So, think back over your employment history, or your time at university or school, or while doing voluntary work or helping out at a sports club. Make a list of some key achievements: goals you reached; people you persuaded; times when you showed bravery or resilience, flexibility or sound organisational skills. Try to make sure they would be relevant to potential employers, though they don't necessarily have to be work based. Use the eight competencies detailed on pages 55–57 as a checklist if that helps. Ask yourself the following questions:

- What was the situation?
- What was my specific part in it?
- What went well?
- What was the result?

When you've got some examples, practise writing them down in no more than 20 words. This is going to help when you come to writing that excellent CV.

Putting it all together

We started this step with the concept of 'Brand You' and suggested that it comprised your values, your skills and strengths as demonstrated by your achievements and your 'core essence' – the Unique Selling Points (USPs) that make you stand out from the crowd. The time you have taken to go through this journey of discovery will put you at a distinct advantage over other applicants who have not considered why a particular employer should employ them. The basic rule is: if *you* don't understand and talk about your values, skills, strengths and achievements, who will?

Having a clear idea of your 'core essence' is the part that pulls all this together. Think about what your values, skills, strengths and achievements say about you. One question I was once asked in an interview was: 'What do we get if we employ you?' It's a great question. Thinking about my core essence really helped me to answer that question clearly and succinctly.

So, the final task for you in this step is to write that 'core essence' paragraph. Take the elevator pitch we mentioned in Step 1 as your starting point. Ask yourself the question I was asked above and write your answer in the language which organisations want to hear.

Key take-aways

Think about the things you will take away from Step 3 and how you will implement them.

Topic	Take-away	Implementation
Creating 'Brand You'	• Brands apply to people as well as products. • They are a shortcut to selling my skills and strengths. • My brand comprises my values, skills and strengths and my 'core essence'.	• Think about what brands say about products. • Refresh my memory of my core values. • Behave in accordance with my brand — it's who I am.
Identifying your strengths		
Identifying your standout three strengths		
Identifying your transferable skills		
Understanding task and people competencies		
Describing your achievements		
Putting it all together: your 'core essence'		

Step 4
WRITE A KILLER CV

'What is written without effort is in general read without pleasure.' — Samuel Johnson (1709–1784), writer and poet

Five ways to succeed

- Tailor your CV to each job you apply for.
- Use action-oriented language, not passive, throughout.
- Match your key skills and strengths to the advert.
- Write an excellent, tailored, covering letter.
- Check spelling, grammar, punctuation and presentation.

Five ways to fail

- Write one CV and use it for every job application.
- Don't bother to check for spelling mistakes.
- Focus on your employment history instead of what the employer wants.
- Make your CV look unique using unusual fonts and colours.
- Email your CV without a covering letter.

The importance of an excellent CV and covering letter

Anyone who has had to look through countless CVs when shortlisting candidates for a vacancy becomes very quickly aware of one thing: most people don't take the time to write a truly excellent CV. Put yourself in the shoes of a hiring manager for a second. If all you have is a CV and covering letter to go on in order to distinguish between scores of candidates, then your first impression of that CV and letter is what makes all the difference. It's the difference between being shortlisted and invited for interview, and being consigned to the waste bin!

Your CV (curriculum vitae, or 'course of life' in Latin) is therefore your first opportunity to market yourself. It tells the employer who you are before they've had the chance to meet you. If you don't get it right then you probably won't get a second opportunity. There's no point in having finely tuned interviewing skills (see Step 5) if you never get to an interview because of a poor CV.

An excellent CV is organic: it's a working document that changes as you change and, as we'll see, should vary according to who you're sending it to.

Tailoring your CV and covering letter

It used to be common practice to send out a single version of your CV to a number of potential employers. That simply doesn't work any more. As we saw in the last step, it's important to talk the language a particular organisation uses – often in terms of competencies – so you need to tailor your CV to the company and the specific vacancy you're applying for.

You can certainly have a 'base' CV that you then adapt; it would be nonsense to start from scratch every time. It's the subtle changes in language, skills and achievements that will say to an employer: this person understands us and what we're looking for. Recruitment consultants and hiring managers are busy people and will make quick decisions (usually in less than a minute) based on the first page of your CV. It not only has to grab their interest in terms of style, presentation and layout, it also has to make the link between the skills, strengths, and sometimes specific experience and what they're looking for.

You can go one step further: it will really make the difference to them if you can repeat exactly the words they use in the job advert. If they're asking for excellent administrative skills then don't assume that mentioning your planning and organising abilities will automatically get that across. Spell it out to them using the exact words they have used so they don't have to second-guess. And you can only do this if you have a different version of your CV for every job you apply for.

Types of CV

There are generally two types of CVs that you can use:

■ **Chronological/Experience-based**

This is a CV that lists your experience and qualifications, with your most recent history first. This may be useful if you have substantial and continuous employment in a particular field as it will highlight your relevant experience, and as such should mainly be used in applications for more specialist jobs.

■ **Skills/Qualifications-based**

This type of CV directs the reader to the relevant transferable skills and qualifications required for the specific vacancy. It's therefore more targeted as it will use the language and specifics of the job, and make good use of non-work related experience such as voluntary or leisure activities, and reduce the impact of gaps in your employment history. For these reasons, this is the most suitable type of CV for most people and is becoming increasingly popular as it allows the employer to instantly see the match between the applicant and the job.

Sounding pro: A skills/qualifications-based CV

Alex Johnson
14 Acacia Avenue, Seachester, SC4 6YH
Tel: 06776 554533
Email: ajohnson@abinternet.com

Personal profile

A web-design graduate with four years' relevant experience in both the public (local government) and private sectors. Specific experience relevant to this role includes designing an intranet website and training employees in its use. Key strengths include teamworking and communication skills.

Key skills and achievements

1 Teamworking: Supported a team of six people to achieve complete data input on in-house system over a period of three weeks. Played an active role by regularly updating the supervisor on progress and offering to take on others' work. On three occasions gave constructive feedback to team members to improve processes.

2 Communication skills: Designed and wrote Seacrest's intranet website using Wordpress 2.0 within the deadline agreed and to budget and with excellent feedback from the customer. Designed and delivered training to key stakeholders to enable them to use and maintain the system. Key strengths applied were: attention to detail, creativity, and results focus.

Experience

June 2011 – Present: *Web Designer* Seacrest Ltd, Brighton
Key responsibilities include design and roll out of company intranet, training of key staff and writing online instruction manual.
July 2008 – June 2011: *Web Design Assistant* Office of Fair Trading, London
Key responsibilities included data gathering and assisting web designers with coding using Wordpress 2.0; sourcing photographic images; creating and monitoring/administering the company's Facebook and Twitter presence.

Education and training

University of London: *BA Hons (2.1) Web Design*; 2008
IT Training Ltd: *Understanding and Using Wordpress 2.0*; 2009

Building your CV

Let's take the various components of this format one at a time to enable you to build your own CV.

Personal details

Simply put your name, address, contact number, personal email address and personal website, if you have one. Do not include anything else such as marital status, number of dependents, age, etc. or the words *Curriculum Vitae*. Simple, uncluttered and clear is the best approach.

Personal profile

At the end of Step 3 you wrote your refined 'core essence' paragraph, which included your values, skills and strengths. This is the starting point for your personal profile statement. If you've done this thoroughly, writing your personal profile should be straightforward. And remember: what you say here may mean the difference between a potential employer reading the rest of your CV or not.

Again, the essence of your personal profile will remain fairly stable; you will have to amend it, however, for each job you apply for to make sure that the language, your experience and key attributes are finely tuned to each specific role and organisation. Look at the key words in the job description or advert, e.g. *retail, marketing, sales, administration*, and make sure you use those words.

Also look for key experiences or qualifications needed, e.g. a graduate degree or specific sector experience and, if you have them, mention them.

In general, your personal profile should be no more than two or three sentences and between 50 and 70 words. Be professional and business-focused. Avoid over-used generic words like *dynamic* or *conscientious*, and remove all pronouns completely; do not use 'I' or, even worse, refer to yourself by name. Finally, remember: this is your only chance to make a good first impression, so fine-tuning this opening paragraph is really worth the effort.

Have a look at this example. What's wrong with it?

> *I am an incredibly motivated individual who would be a great asset to your organisation. I have a number of key skills and dynamic attributes which make me stand out from the rest. My communication skills are second to none and I feel I would be able to take your organisation to unparalleled success.*

There are several things wrong with this personal profile:

■ The emphasis on 'I' suggests it is all about the individual, not the organisation.

■ It has too many meaningless or clichéd descriptions: *motivated, dynamic, second to none.*

■ It has a rather arrogant feel.

■ It's generic. It could apply to virtually any job.

■ The specific skills and attributes needed for the job are not mentioned.

Now look at this example. What's good about it?

> *A web-design graduate with four years' relevant experience in both the public (local government) and private sectors. Specific experience relevant to this role includes designing an intranet website and training employees in its use. Key strengths include an attention to detail, a focus on results and relationship management.*

This personal profile has the following strengths:

■ It's professional, business-like and concisely written.

■ Key strengths and relevant experience are mentioned specifically.

■ Number of years' relevant experience is immediately clarified.

■ Two sectors are mentioned.

If you're applying for your first job

There is one more thing you need to consider: if you're applying for your first job, you'll obviously have little directly relevant experience to mention. Be specific about your transferable skills and strengths, but in addition you could mention your career aspirations – something not normally recommended as this is a personal thing. This will say something about your future thinking and your ambitions. If you have a longer term plan that's relevant to the job being advertised or the organisation you're applying to, then include it in your personal profile too.

Over to you

Write a personal profile that you can keep and use as a template for adapting to a variety of vacancies. Make sure it captures the 'core essence' of you!

Key skills and achievements

It's now time to remind yourself of your key skills and strengths and to think of examples from your work history or other experiences that demonstrate them; in other words, your achievements. When did you last demonstrate your planning and organising skills, for example? What was the scenario? What specifically did you do? What was the result? What feedback did you receive, if any? Remind yourself of some of those key achievements and write them down in a concise format. Write them all down; you can choose which particular ones to include depending on the job itself.

Most people tend to choose the three or four most relevant achievements for the specific role they're applying for. This gives enough information to make it clear how you meet the criteria the employer is looking for without overwhelming the reader with too much detail.

Now look through the job section of a newspaper or website and find a job advertisement that interests you. Look at the advertisement and ask yourself the following questions:

■ What are the most important skills mentioned? If you can, try to determine an order of importance.

■ How can you match your own key strengths and skills onto those mentioned?

■ How can you make your previous achievements relevant to this job?

Your use of language is important when writing examples of your key skills and achievements. Adjectives such as *talented, motivated* and *dynamic* are meaningless and can sound like arrogance. Using verbs (action-oriented words) like *achieved, influenced, developed, coordinated, managed, increased, reduced, scheduled, solved, planned, analysed, delivered* makes your writing sound positive and proactive, and communicates energy. Use the relevant tense: past for previous jobs; present for your current job.

Future employers will want to know both the 'what' and the 'how', i.e. what you achieved and what you did, or what skills and strengths you demonstrated, to make success happen. It's not enough to simply say *I achieved this*. You need to say *I achieved this outcome by doing that and that, using these skills and drawing on this key strength*. Instead of simply providing a list of duties for each role you've had, focus on what successes you've achieved. Use three or four of the most relevant skills/achievements in this format if you can:

■ First, mention your most relevant competency or skill for this particular vacancy, using competency-based language or the key words and phrases used in the job advert. Remind yourself of the type of language used from the section on competencies in Step 3 on pages 55–57. Then follow with your next most relevant skill, and so on.

■ Illustrate each skill with examples of any achievements you have from your past that relate to the skill. This is so you can provide directly relevant evidence to someone who you can't explain these to in person. Don't forget to mention each successful outcome.

Here are some examples:

Teamworking: *Supported a team of six people to achieve complete data input on in-house system over a period of three weeks. Played an active role by regularly updating the supervisor on progress and completion of tasks and offering to take on others' work. On three occasions gave constructive feedback to team members to improve processes.*

Communication skills: *Designed and wrote Seacrest's intranet website using Wordpress 2.0 within the deadline agreed and to budget and with excellent feedback from the customer. Designed and delivered training to key stakeholders within Seacrest to enable them to use and maintain the system. Key strengths applied were: attention to detail, creativity and results focus.*

Client relationship:

■ *Responded to 100% of customer enquiries within the target of 24 hours.*

■ *Maintained the quality of calls as measured by customer feedback.*

■ *Nominated for call centre employee of the month in both July and August 2013.*

■ *Subsequently requested by management to train new staff in client relationship management.*

Experience

This section should be a summary of your work history. Make sure that you mention all relevant work and other activities. Part-time work, short-term contracts, voluntary work, and any committees or working groups you took part in during your studies; these are all valid. An employer wants to see what you've spent your time doing. If you have gaps in your work history, fill them with examples of activities that have added to your skills and achievements; this way you can demonstrate your enthusiasm and proactivity. This could include reading, voluntary work or writing a blog.

Once you've identified the key competencies and skills required for the job, giving examples of outcomes and successes as we've just discussed, then this part of your CV may be quite brief and in the form of a list, starting with the most recent first. Present each example in the following format: date; job title; location; key responsibilities.

June 2011 – Present: Web Designer Seacrest Ltd, Brighton
Key responsibilities include design and roll out of company intranet, training of key staff and writing online instruction manual.

July 2008 – June 2011: Web Design Assistant Office of Fair Trading, London
Key responsibilities included data gathering and assisting web designers with coding using Wordpress 2.0; sourcing photographic images; creating and monitoring/administering the company's Facebook and Twitter presence.

Sept 2006 – May 2008: Volunteer Newchester under 14s football team
Key responsibilities included arranging all kit maintenance and washing; communicating match arrangements to all parties and mentoring several players.

Education and training

In this section, briefly list your qualifications and any relevant training or development activities. Again, list these in reverse order, with the most recent first. However, if you have higher-level academic qualifications such as a Bachelor's or Master's degree, you may prefer to highlight these in a separate section and then list additional training or qualifications afterwards for greater impact. Employers want to see evidence of continuous learning and development, so make sure you mention any training that may relate to a specific job.

If you're fresh from school and looking for your first or second job, then provide details of the schools you attended and subjects you studied, as well as the level of qualifications taken and grades attained. Once you start applying for more senior roles or have a degree, then you don't need to mention your school-based qualifications such as GCSEs or A levels.

Finally, only mention hobbies and interests (in a separate section) if they're relevant to the job or if they provide examples of your skills and strengths.

Final considerations

Finally, we need to consider presentation. The best CV can be completely ruined by typing errors and the way it looks, so follow these guidelines to make sure it appears professional:

■ Keep it brief. Most CVs should be no more than two pages of A4 paper in length.

■ Think about how it looks on a screen and also when printed out. Some documents look fine when you're creating them, but look too busy and cluttered when printed.

■ Use clean, modern fonts such as Arial, Helvetica, Verdana or Calibri. Fonts such as Times New Roman look increasingly old-fashioned; never use funny or elaborate fonts such as Comic Sans! Make sure you're consistent and use the same font throughout.

■ Most people use font sizes of 10 or 11 point (with slightly larger headings) to allow for easy reading. Any smaller and your CV will be difficult to read; any larger and you may not be able to fit enough detail into your two pages.

■ Avoid any distracting clutter or styling variations. Keep it clean, with gaps, margins and spacing, and keep your use of italics and bold to a minimum. You could bold company names, competency headings and key qualifications, for example, and put the job title in italics.

■ Finally, check it, check it again and then get it checked by someone else! Any spelling, grammatical or punctuation mistakes will be noticed and will be a black mark against you. Even a single mistake gives a very unprofessional impression. Don't rely merely on spellchecking software.

The covering letter

If your CV is about selling *you*, then your covering letter is about selling your CV. It may determine whether your CV gets read at all, so it's worth spending some time exploring the qualities of a good covering letter. You should write one even if one is not specifically asked for; it may help you stand out from the crowd and ensure your CV gets read.

Of course, many job applications these days are made electronically – by email with attachments. The covering letter in these circumstances would normally form the body of your email. It certainly doesn't hurt to write it as a letter as well and attach that as '[Your name] covering letter.docx' or similar, as some companies like to file all correspondence as Microsoft Word or pdf documents.

In the same way as the CV, and just as importantly, the covering letter should be tailored to the specific job applied for. By all means have a couple of templates at the ready, but organisations will spot a mass-produced letter immediately.

Your covering letter, then, is the means by which you get your CV noticed. It should be well written, brief – one side of A4 or around 200 words – and make the reader want to know more about you.

Structuring your covering letter

Good covering letters often follow a three-paragraph rule, something like this:

- Opening paragraph – a longer version of your elevator pitch

- Middle paragraph – outlining key achievements and experience relevant to the vacancy, together with other relevant information and what you can offer the role

- Closing paragraph – a 'thank you for considering this application' statement

Greeting and signing off

You may have the name of the person you're writing to. If you don't, it's worth making the effort to find out. Telephone the organisation to find out the best person to send your application to, or visit the company website. It's convention to address them using *Dear …* followed by their surname. On the next line, state the job vacancy you're applying for.

Finally, when signing off, follow the rule that if you haven't addressed it to someone specifically, i.e. you've used *Dear Sir or Madam*, then use *Yours faithfully*. If you addressed the person by name, use *Yours sincerely*.

The opening paragraph

Your opening paragraph is essentially a longer version of your elevator pitch or personal profile from your CV. It should mention why you're writing and should immediately grab the attention of the reader to make them want to read more. If you've been introduced to the person you're addressing by a mutual contact, or are writing in response to a specific advertisement, mention this here. Your personality can shine a little bit more than in the more formal constraints of your CV, so aim for a balance between warm and personable, and yet professional.

The middle paragraph

This part of your letter is where you should highlight your key achievements and qualifications, and the skills and strengths that make you suitable for this role. Do not just cut and paste from your CV. Instead, take the three or four key elements from the advert and/or job description and spell out how you match their requirements and how you can help them.

Here's another example of addressing key criteria the employer is looking for:

> *I notice from your advertisement that training colleagues in the use of Microsoft Office is a key part of this role. As well as having used the full software package for over five years, I have trained over 100 people in the use of Word and PowerPoint over the last 24 months, and 50 people in the use of Excel during the same period – all with excellent feedback. All training courses were written by myself.*

The closing paragraph

Finally, you need to end your letter with a 'thank you for taking the time' to read your letter, and adding that you would be delighted to be invited for an interview and the opportunity to discuss your application further. Finish with something like *I look forward to hearing from you.*

There is an example of a good covering letter on the next page.

Sounding pro: The covering letter

Alex Johnson
14 Acacia Avenue
Seachester
SC4 6YH

Mr G. Jones
Milton Associates
76 Trading Estate
Brighton, BN98 7FR

7th June 2014

Dear Mr Jones,

Re: Job vacancy reference number 345/998 – Web Design Assistant

I am writing in response to the advertisement placed in the Brighton Evening Echo relating to the above vacancy. I was recommended to you by Deepa Aggarwal, one of your key suppliers, who felt that my skills and experience would make me a suitable candidate for this role. I have four years' experience in a very similar role, gained after achieving my degree in web design at UCL, and I am excited by the additional experience this particular vacancy would afford me.

One of the key requirements of my current role is being fully conversant with Wordpress 2.0, which I notice is also an essential requirement of this vacancy. I have used Wordpress 2.0 for the last three years and now train other colleagues in its use. Over the last three years I have successfully designed some 15 websites using this software, with excellent feedback.

Thank you very much for taking the time to consider my application. This position is of great interest to me and will enable me to consolidate and further build on my existing experience. I feel I could add value to this role and to your organisation.

Yours sincerely,
Alex Johnson

Attachment: CV

Final considerations

As with the CV, presentation is everything, so follow these guidelines to make sure your covering letter looks both professional and consistent with your CV:

■ Keep it to one page of A4.

■ Use the letter heading conventions illustrated on the opposite page. Start with your address in the top right-hand corner, followed by the recipient's name and address below and justified to the left. Justify the date to the right. Don't forget to insert a heading in bold to stand out from the rest of the text.

■ Again, use clean, modern fonts such as Arial, Helvetica, Verdana or Calibri and 10 or 11 point.

■ Most importantly, don't forget to check it for errors!

Finally, remember the essential rule of writing your CV and covering letter: they're sales tools, and therefore need to be tailored to every single job you apply for. The extra effort is worth it – it will help you get to the next stage of job hunting – the interview!

Key take-aways

Think about the things you will take away from Step 4 and how you will implement them.

Topic	Take-away	Implementation
The importance of having an excellent CV and covering letter	• *Creates the first impression.* • *It's my first marketing or selling opportunity.* • *It's often the only way of securing an interview.*	• *Put the time aside to write some practice or template CVs and covering letters.*
How to tailor CVs and covering letters for specific jobs		
Deciding which type of CV to use		
How to write a personal profile		
How to write the *Personal details* section of a CV		
How to write the *Skills and achievements* section of a CV		
How to write the *Experience* section of a CV		
How to write the *Education and training* section of a CV		
How to write a covering letter		

Step 5

ACE THE INTERVIEW

'Talking and eloquence are not the same: to speak, and to speak well, are two things.'
— Ben Jonson (1572–1637), poet and playwright

Five ways to succeed

- Recognise that an interview is your opportunity to shine.
- Do your preparation thoroughly.
- Present yourself appropriately.
- As much as you can, relax.
- Rehearse lots of examples of past competencies and successes.

Five ways to fail

- Assume the job is already yours.
- Go with a 'they can take me or leave me' attitude.
- Give long answers – the longer the better.
- Be disparaging about your old employer and colleagues.
- Arrive late.

What is an interview for?

So, you've submitted an excellent CV and covering letter and have been invited for an interview. Congratulations! You wouldn't have got this far if you hadn't spent time making sure that your transferable skills and strengths were relevant to the particular job. Companies don't waste their time inviting people in for interview if they don't think that they may be a suitable candidate for the role. Everything you've done so far has got them interested, so now your job is to impress them face-to-face. Essentially, that is what an interview is for.

Despite the fact that the interview is actually not a particularly good way of assessing someone's suitability for a job (we'll look at this idea in more detail in Step 6), it's virtually unheard of for someone to be employed without having an interview. It appears to be the unwritten rule of recruitment! Interviews take many forms and structures; some are good, some are bad, but as far as you're concerned, being prepared is the key. This step will make sure you attend your interview with confidence and knowledge about what you'll be asked to do.

Interviews have changed somewhat over the last few years. Increasingly, companies are moving away from asking vague questions relating to how you might deal with fictitious scenarios, mainly because the interviewee can simply make it up. Instead, questions are often focused on what you have actually done in the past; what you did, what worked, what didn't, what you learned and what the result was. It's far harder to make up this 'evidence' and you can prepare best by having a set of answers ready.

In Step 3, we used competencies as a kind of shorthand for second-guessing what an employer is looking for; by doing so when preparing for an interview you will come across as prepared and confident – and a good match for the job itself. We will look at these competency-based questions in more detail later in this step.

So far, you've put down on paper (or electronically) your skills, strengths, experience, etc. in a fairly standard format, and this has been used as a filtering device by those doing the hiring. They'll be asking themselves whether you fit the required profile for the job: whether what you put down matches what they want. The interview, on the other hand, is an opportunity for you *both* to get to know each other. In addition to your answers to their questions and looking at the way you've presented yourself, the interviewers will be asking themselves about cultural fit: *Would this person fit in here? Will they thrive in this environment? What value will they add?* Recruiting is an expensive business, so they'll want to satisfy themselves that you're serious about the job and serious about them. The interview will give you the chance to explain your CV, to give examples of your skills and strengths, and to ask questions about the role and the organisation. It's your opportunity to shine! And shining means selling yourself in the best possible light.

The message here, then, is that interviewers are looking at both the practical side of things, such as skills, experience and the like, and also the more intangible 'feeling' side: *How has he/she come across interpersonally?* And, rightly or wrongly: *How does he/she look?* And crucially: *Do we like him/her?*

Types of interview

In order to know what to expect, it's useful to be aware of the different types of interview that are commonly used by organisations. If the organisation you've applied to conforms to best practice, they'll normally tell you in advance what the process is like and who'll be interviewing you (and any variations such as whether Skype™ or video-conferencing will be used), together with any assessments they may ask you to undertake. We'll look at the range of possible assessments and how to survive them in Step 6.

The panel interview

It's usual for the interview to be conducted by two or more interviewers. This is actually a good thing as it takes away an element of individual interviewer bias. Interviewers have their favourites and will pick and choose what they notice – both good things and bad things! The interviewers will be acting as a check on each other, so you're less likely to be asked inappropriate or unhelpful questions. Ensure you get the opportunity to use their names and to greet each person individually. If you haven't been told their names in advance, it's OK to ask. You'll often be asked set questions by each panel member, so remember to address your answer to them in particular, but don't forget to periodically sweep the panel with your eyes so you keep everyone's interest.

The one-to-one interview

Sometimes, and not very often these days, you may have an interview with just one interviewer. When this type of interview is used, it's usually as a form of preliminary 'warm-up' or sometimes even informal conversation about the role, the company and your past history. They will probably simply ask you to clarify points on your CV and try to find out a little bit more about you and what your aspirations are.

The second interview

Some organisations' recruitment processes incorporate just the one interview. Usually, however, it's a two-stage process in which the first interview is designed to check the validity and accuracy of your CV and to decide if they (and you) are prepared to take your application further. This second interview is designed to probe deeper and further into the specific skills and attributes the role requires and whether you can provide evidence for them.

The HR interview

Some organisations include a separate process conducted by their Human Resources department. If not, it's likely that a member of HR will sit in on the panel interview itself. The HR interview is designed to check more general suitability and employability at a level somewhat divorced from the job itself – in effect, an independent reality check. Be prepared to repeat answers you gave at previous interviews and, if relevant, for questions about your eligibility to work in the country.

Do your research

You will have done some research into the company and job which you're applying for in order to tailor your CV, so the first stage of interview preparation is to refresh your memory with what the organisation does and what the job is designed to achieve. Make sure you look through the company website and familiarise yourself with names and faces, values and any challenges currently facing the organisation. You may also want to research into their key suppliers and/or customers, and also their key competitors. If you can mention the names of major competitors or suppliers, or mention the fact that you know their core values, you will be demonstrating that you have taken the time to do your homework, which will never fail to impress.

If you know the names of the people who will be interviewing you, do an internet search or a LinkedIn search for them. What's their background? Remember that they'll probably be doing the same about you, so make sure there's nothing out there in the virtual world that you don't want a prospective interviewer to see.

Finally, if you know anyone who works in the organisation or has worked there in the past, have a chat with them to discuss the company culture. What's it like to work there? What staff survey results have there been? What advice are they able to give you – and do they know your interviewers?

Dressing for the interview

Dressing appropriately for an interview may seem like common sense, but so many people get it wrong. The impression we give someone in the first few seconds of meeting someone new tends to become the way we're viewed from that point on. Context is also important: if you're going for an administrative role in a typical company, then it's difficult to go wrong with a dark business suit, for both men and women. If it's a creative company (such as media, advertising or some technology companies), then it may be appropriate to be more individual in your dress.

And one more thing: don't forget personal grooming. Interviewers will notice personal hygiene, cleanliness of hair and clothes and whether you've polished your shoes! It's also important to be comfortable in what you wear – pain can be very distracting!

At the interview

Body language

Interviewers will be looking at the way you're dressed and they will also be looking at how you're behaving. Of course, most interviewers will expect candidates for a job to be a little nervous, but again, first impressions count. The impression you want to give is one of being calm, confident and controlled with some added warmth.

Think of it as being assertive – a mid-point between being submissive and shy at one end and aggressive and arrogant at the other. Being assertive means being polite, comfortable in your own skin (it will help if you're comfortable in what you're wearing, too!) and, in short, being 'you'. As soon as you try to over-sell yourself or start putting on an act, you're in danger of tipping over into sounding arrogant. Interviewers will be judging you right from the first second they meet you, so have this assertive image in your head.

So how do we give off this impression of being calm and confident? While it's partly about the words we say, it's usually more to do with the way we say those words and what our body is doing while we say them.

Think about the messages these behaviours give:

- **Your smile:** It's the first thing they'll notice, so even if it's the last thing you feel like doing, give a warm, open, friendly smile. Practise in the mirror!

- **Your handshake:** This is a vital part of that important first impression, so make it firm (but not too firm) while looking directly at them and smiling. You also need to be aware of cultural differences, so if you're applying for work outside the UK, then some research into handshaking customs would be useful. In the UK, wait for the interviewer to offer their hand, then give up to two pumps of the arm clearly and confidently.

- **Eye contact:** Again, balance is the key here. You don't want to avoid eye contact as that gives the impression of lacking confidence or even feeling guilty about something, and neither do you want to stare maniacally at them. When your interviewer is speaking, give lots of eye contact – say 90 per cent of the time; when you're speaking, aim for at least 50 per cent.

- **Listening behaviour:** Demonstrate you're listening in addition to giving plenty of eye contact, by periodically nodding, giving little responses such as 'Yes, I see' and 'Of course, yes', and don't forget that smile!

- **Your body:** Keep a nice, upright posture, with your feet on the ground or crossed at the ankle. Try not to fidget. Sit back, but upright, in your chair, as opposed to perching on the front of it – otherwise you'll look nervous.

Dealing with nerves

I remember once attending a training session on good presentation skills. One key piece of advice has stayed with me: that being nervous can be a good thing, so learn to appreciate it. What the presenter meant was that nerves are a natural response to a stressful situation, and as long as they're not going into overdrive, can help us remain sharp and focused. It might not feel like that at the time, however, so let's look at some strategies for dealing with those nerves.

■ Help yourself by planning your journey to the interview in advance. Do a practice run if you're unsure of where to go, and get your clothes ready the evening before. Arrive early.

■ Try to stop those negative thoughts as soon as they start appearing. Many of us will have some self-limiting beliefs such as 'I'm useless at interviews' or 'If I'm not perfect, I'll fail.' As soon as they appear, change them into something else or challenge them. Tell yourself that you've been invited to interview for a reason and that others will be thinking the same as you. And no one you're up against will be perfect, so you don't need to be either. Practise doing what athletes do before a big event: replace the negative thoughts with 'You can do it' and 'You're well prepared, so you have as much chance as anyone' and 'You have the skills and experience to succeed in this role.'

■ Think back to the strengths you identified in Step 2. Think about how you can consciously and meaningfully engage them at the interview. What we mean here is to purposely turn the dial up on them. Do you have a relationship-building strength, or a common-sense strength, for example? How can you engage them right now? Sometimes, just being conscious about doing so is enough.

■ Put things into perspective. Ask yourself: 'What's the worst that could happen?' Tell yourself that if you don't get this opportunity, there will be others. Recognise that interviewing is a two-way process – you're interviewing them too and you can always choose to walk away if the job or organisation doesn't feel right.

■ Don't forget to breathe. The more you engage in deep breathing, the more you will generate alpha waves in your brain which serve to calm you down. Just before your interview, breathe in to a count of six and out to a count of ten. Do this ten times and notice how much more relaxed you feel.

■ Finally, try to visualise success. Again, many elite athletes use this technique; they may 'watch' themselves in their head crossing a finish line first, imagining the roar of the crowd and how they feel to have won. Practise this technique:

1 Give yourself some uninterrupted free time with no distractions. Ten minutes should do it.

2 Imagine yourself in the interview, and watch yourself being calm and confident when greeting the panel members. Notice the fact that you're smiling and that they are too.

3 Imagine yourself sitting down in the chair, looking forward to the questions you're about to face because you know you'll be able to answer them and come across at your best.

4 Watch as you answer their questions and notice that the panel members are smiling and nodding as you answer them.

5 See yourself being offered the role and notice how it feels.

6 Run it through several times in your head – and every time you start to feel nervous, play it again!

Answering interview questions

So far in this step, we've focused on body language, how to present yourself and how to deal with nerves. All of these are important, as interviewers will be making very quick decisions about your suitability – as we've said, the first impression you make counts hugely. However, all this will count for nothing if you're unable to answer the panel's questions. Whatever question you're answering, follow these three basic principles:

■ Keep your answers brief and to the point.

■ Answer the question you're being asked.

■ Give evidence and show results – explain what you did and what happened.

Before we get to specific interview questions, let's think about the language we use and the way we should talk in interviews.

Using positive language

You will remember in Step 4 (Write a killer CV) that we mentioned how important the language we use is. We focused on action words which sound positive, dynamic and focused on the successes you have achieved. Exactly the same principles apply in an interview situation too. You need to sound confident in what you're saying and create the impression that you are a credible potential employee.

In addition, follow these guidelines;

■ Don't litter your sentences with 'fillers' such as *er, very, quite, sort of, you know, I mean.*

■ Don't use words like *try* or *I would do my best.* Be confident and positive by using *will* instead.

■ Be modest but not too modest. You need to say what you're good at and give examples, but don't exaggerate or boast. Remember the advice earlier on the difference between being assertive and arrogant.

■ Never use management speak or jargon. The interviewers will have heard it all before and may think you're using it to hide the fact that you don't know the answer.

■ Don't make your answers so vague as to be meaningless. The best answers are short, sharp and clear – and actually answer the question asked.

It's not just what you say; it's how you say it

The *way* we speak is just as important as the words we use. If you have a strong regional accent, or if English is an additional language, then pay attention to whether your interviewers ask you to repeat yourself, and make a concerted effort to speak more clearly. Always pose your responses as an answer, not a question. We'll discuss this in more detail in the next step when we look at presenting, but if you have a tendency to raise the intonation at the end of each sentence, it gives the impression that you're asking a question and makes you sound rather passive. Make an effort to go down at the end of the sentence, not up – unless you're actually asking a question, of course!

Step 5: Ace the interview

How to answer three classic opening questions

Many interviews start with some general, open questions which are designed to get you more relaxed and in interview mode. Don't be fooled into thinking that your answers to these opening questions don't matter – not many interviewers bother to ask questions that aren't used to assess you in some way.

■ *Tell us about yourself*

This is often the opening question. There's nothing wrong with mentioning one or two personal things about yourself to start, but really this is your opportunity to give your best 'elevator pitch'. If you mention your current role, you must make the link obvious with this particular job and the qualities you possess which will add value to their organisation.

■ *Why do you want to work for us?*

They are really asking why them in particular, as opposed to any other organisation. This is where you have an opportunity to demonstrate that you've done some research about the company. Mention its aims and strategy if you know them, its reputation or recent exciting growth or innovative products, or that it was specifically recommended to you. Remember that they want to hear why you're drawn to them, not why you want to leave your current employer.

■ *Why should we employ you?*

Typical variations of this question are: *What do we get if we hire you?* or *What are your key strengths?* If you've identified your key skills and strengths in Step 3, then any of these questions is a gift! And you will be able to give examples too.

Competency-based questions

We introduced competencies in Step 3 as a way of understanding the language that employers use and want to hear. In interviews you will be asked for examples of when you last demonstrated a competency which is important for the new role. Again, your preparation in Step 3 will help you enormously here. When interviewers ask competency-based questions, they're actually asking for a story; a story about your past that tells them whether they want you in their future. You need to give them the evidence!

The principle behind competency-based questioning is that the past is the best predictor of the future; if you can demonstrate that you've used that skill before, you'll be able to do it again. Often, the competency area being assessed will be made very explicit. An interviewer may say: 'We would like to ask some questions around the area of planning and organising', and this is your cue to get ready to give an example of when you demonstrated your planning and organising skills.

Remember that they'll be writing your answers down, so help them by making your answers brief and to the point. Take care to actually answer the question they ask explicitly and don't forget to describe both the scenario itself and the positive outcome that you made possible.

Answering those difficult questions

While it's not the purpose of an interview to catch you out, some questions are designed to be tricky to answer. Let's finish with some examples of these difficult questions – and some suggestions as to how to answer them.

■ *What are your weaknesses?*

This is about balance. If you give a whole list of weaknesses, you'll appear unemployable. If you give the impression that you don't have any, it may make you appear arrogant. The approach to aim for is to be honest with one or two potential weaknesses (or a strength over-used) and to give an example of how you have mitigated it. For example, you could say: 'My strength in being strategically minded means that sometimes I can let go of the detail. Now I've recognised this, I make sure I get important documents checked thoroughly.'

■ *What's wrong with your current employer/job?*

Remember that it's never a good idea to criticise past employers or jobs. Your answer could tactfully suggest that while there is nothing wrong with them or it, you're looking for a fresh challenge and new opportunities to learn. For example: 'I had been doing the same job for a couple of years and was concerned that I might be getting stale. I raised this with my boss, who wasn't able to give me any assurances that the job would develop in the foreseeable future, so I felt, with regret, that it was time to move on.' There is absolutely nothing wrong with owning up to being made redundant, incidentally.

■ *Do you have any questions for us?*

This is your cue that the interview is coming to an end. If you have no questions for them, it may make you appear as if you haven't prepared for the interview. Instead, treat this as an opportunity to show your proactivity and resourcefulness – but keep it to two or three at the most. Never ask about salary or other benefits at this stage. Examples of good closing questions are:

- What do you see as the key challenges in the first few months for this job?
- Is there anything about my application that I can help to clarify?
- How would you describe the culture of this organisation?
- What is the next step in the process?

Sounding pro

Here are some examples of answers to common interview questions:

Answering opening questions

Q: Why do you want to work for us?
A: *I love your products, I use them myself and would like to be a part in your continued success. I also notice that you're expanding into the overseas market and that sounds very exciting.*

Answering competency-based questions

Q: Tell us about a time when you had to perform under pressure.
A: *I was a training course administrator and I had to deal with a situation where the trainer was taken ill on the morning of the event. There were 16 people about to attend the course so, first of all, I got an alternative date from the training provider, then I contacted all the delegates by email notifying them of the last-minute cancellation. I also phoned or left messages where I could, sent a message on Twitter, and put a notice on the door.*

Q: What was the result?
A: *In the end, only two people didn't get the message. I met them in the room, apologised and offered the alternative date.*

Answering difficult questions

Q: What are your weaknesses?
A: *One of my strengths is attention to detail, and most of the time it works for me. But sometimes, if I'm not careful, I can miss a deadline as I want everything to be perfect – I've had to learn to rein this tendency in!*

Key take-aways

Think about the things you will take away from Step 5 and how you will implement them.

Topic	Take-away	Implementation
Understanding what an interview is for	• *Recognise that it's about selling myself.* • *Congratulate myself on getting this far.* • *Preparation is key.*	• *Practise my elevator pitch.* • *Have a ready-made stock of examples from the past.* • *Remind myself of my key skills and strengths.*
What to expect from the different types of interview		
Dressing for an interview		
Using correct body language		
Dealing with nerves		
Answering opening questions		
Answering competency-based questions		
Answering difficult questions		

Step 6

PERFORM WELL IN ASSESSMENTS

'*There are few things that psychologists agree on, but one of them is that unstructured interviews do not work.*' — Robert Wood and Tim Payne: Competency-Based Recruitment and Selection (1998)

Five ways to succeed

- Understand why companies use assessments.
- Know what to expect from the different types of assessment.
- Practise psychometric tests and presentations.
- Know what assessors are looking for.
- Learn to value – and ask for – feedback.

Five ways to fail

- Assume an interview is all you will be asked to do.
- Play the 'clown' at an assessment centre.
- On no account know what assessments to expect.
- If you don't do well on one assessment, forget the rest.
- Take no notice of feedback.

Why do companies use assessments?

Interviews are the most obvious – and widely used – form of assessment used by recruiters and hiring managers. It's easy to see why: they at least look like they measure what you want them to, i.e. whether a candidate can do the job or not. And not many companies would hire someone they hadn't met – and you probably wouldn't want to work somewhere that hadn't invited you to meet them!

However, as a form of assessment, interviews are in fact not very useful when it comes to predicting whether someone can actually perform the job in question. Interviews often attempt to get to the 'answer': whether you can work as part of a team, for example – by asking you about how you would work in one of their teams. Competency-based interviews, which are more useful, achieve this by asking you to give examples from the past, as we have seen. This works because it's harder to make examples up, and interviewers can usually spot it if you do.

Less rigorous interviews ask what you would do in hypothetical situations. This has less validity because you are, by definition, making it up anyway. Whether you would then actually behave like that if the situation did come about is another matter entirely.

Assessors don't really want to know what you think you would do. So, as we mentioned earlier, as a way of predicting whether someone you don't know can do a job, the interview is not particularly good. A poorly constructed interview with untrained interviewers is only slightly better than chance when predicting job success.

Many companies therefore strive to obtain actual evidence of someone doing a task. This data can then be objectively assessed. This evidence is far better at predicting whether someone could do the job in the future, because you can watch it happening right in front of you.

When a series of different assessments is used in combination, this is often referred to as an *assessment centre*. An assessment centre, therefore, is a set of activities, not a place. While they're extremely rigorous and generally work very well indeed in terms of their ability to select the right person or people for the job, they are labour-intensive and therefore expensive. As a result, they're often only used by larger organisations and during large-scale recruitment drives (for example, graduate entry schemes or key managerial level jobs), where the cost of making poor selection decisions is quite high.

The short answer, then, to why companies use assessments is that they tend to predict who can perform subsequently in the job well. And the typical interview doesn't. Many enlightened companies find that the benefits of using assessments far outweigh the costs.

Types of assessment

Most forms of assessment will look like elements of the job in question or, if this isn't possible, will include something that measures the same competencies. The assessments are chosen precisely to reflect the job, and assessors will be specifically trained in the objective marking of your performance. In best-practice assessment use, you will be told in advance of each exercise precisely which competencies are being assessed – usually three or four per exercise.

Organisations have many assessment options to choose from. The choice is determined by how well a particular exercise measures the competencies required for the job. In the next few pages we'll take a look at the most common forms of assessment you may encounter, and how to perform in them to the best of your ability. Try to remember that each assessment is an opportunity for you to demonstrate in a fair and objective way that you have a particular job-related skill, and that every candidate is going through the same thing.

Even if you don't get the particular job you've applied for, good performance in assessments may sometimes lead to you being classed as an 'also suitable' and may lead to further opportunities with that organisation.

On the next few pages we will look at some of the most common types of assessments.

Psychometric tests

Psychometric tests fall into two broad camps: ability tests and personality questionnaires.

Ability tests

These are designed to measure specific elements of your logical thinking ability, such as verbal or numerical reasoning, or an aspect of intellectual functioning such as spatial awareness. There are right and wrong answers (usually multiple-choice) and your score is the number of correct responses you give in the time available. These tests are timed, so you have to work as quickly and as accurately as you can. Your score will then be compared with the scores of people who have completed the test before, to see where you would fall in the comparison group chosen, e.g. the general population or UK graduates, for example. There are books available where you can practise these types of test. You can also try practice examples at test publishers such as www.shl.com.

SPATIAL
AWARENESS
TEST
START : 9·30
FINISH : 10·00

Personality questionnaires

These are not tests as such as there are no right or wrong answers. They don't measure your abilities, but rather your preferences in terms of the style you might use at work. There are many different models of personality, but the trait-based ones are the ones most commonly used in selection. In these, your personality is divided into a number of traits (such as Rule-consciousness and Persuasiveness), and they assess how your answers compare to the average. There is no time limit to these types of questions, although a likely indication is usually given. You may be asked to complete these questionnaires (often online) in advance of meeting the company concerned, as they often use the data to feed into the interview process. For example, if you scored low on Persuasiveness compared to the general population and were applying for a job as a sales consultant, they might use this information to probe for further evidence to satisfy themselves that you can be persuasive when you need to be.

Useful tips

Here are some useful tips for completing psychometric questionnaires:

- Ability tests are usually timed, so answer quickly. Look at how many questions there are and remember that ability tests are designed so that most people do not quite finish.

- Read the instructions carefully; they're not designed to catch you out but to make sure you do what is required of you.

- You're usually given the opportunity to complete practice examples first. Make sure you understand why you got your answers either right or wrong by asking for clarity from the test administrator.

Role-plays

Many people dread the idea of doing a role-play, but, as with all assessments, it's important to remember two things. First, no one is trying to catch you out; assessments are designed to try to get an objective idea of what you can do, not what you can't. Second, you're not required to act or be someone you're not. The observers are looking for the real you.

A typical role-play scenario is based on a sale or negotiation, dealing with a difficult customer or (for managers) addressing a performance concern with a member of staff. The specific competencies being assessed will obviously reflect the nature of the job you're applying for, even if the scenario does not.

Role-plays are used primarily to assess your interpersonal skills. You are given some time to prepare a scenario, with a situation brief that usually requires no specific knowledge. The person you are meeting is played by an actor, who has also been given a brief. You will then have some specified time to hold a meeting and achieve the outcome mentioned in your brief. The actor will be instructed to be tricky but not impossible to deal with – their responses and demeanour will be a 'real-life' response to the way you're handling the conversation.

Remember that it's not necessarily the content of the actual conversation that's being assessed, but rather the style with which you undertake to resolve the particular issue. Is your communication style clear? Have you structured the conversation? Have you tried hard to get to a meaningful outcome?

The whole performance will be followed by an observer (familiar with the exercise and trained in the art of assessing), who will be looking at your competency in the specific inter-personal skills being measured. These could be influencing and persuading, resolving conflict, verbal communication skills, negotiating, or other sales-based skills. The instructions and your brief should make the specific competencies being measured clear; if they're not, then it's fine to ask. The observer will play no part in the conversation and you should just ignore their presence as much as you can.

Role-plays, then, are an excellent example of the attempt to get first-hand evidence of what you can actually do. You may say at interview that you have excellent negotiation skills, and give lots of evidence to support this claim, but in the role-play the observer can see this in action and will mark your performance (and those of the other candidates) against a set of standard behaviours.

Useful tips

Here are some tips for performing well at role-plays:

■ Make sure you read the brief thoroughly and remember to keep the purpose in mind – it's your style being measured, not merely the end result.

■ Be yourself. The actor is acting, whereas the observer wants to see the real you. Don't play to the observer. It doesn't go down well with the observer if you do comedy asides to them.

■ Use the full time given to prepare the outcome you want from the meeting. How do you think the actor has been briefed to behave? What should you expect? What options do you have to get a successful outcome?

Group exercises

In many ways, group exercises are similar to role-plays. The primary purpose is often not your ability to solve the problem being given to you (although that may form a part of the assessment), but is often to observe how you work in a group. As such, the competencies being assessed are likely to have an interpersonal skills bias, such as influencing and persuading, communication skills, teamworking and possibly leading/facilitating, as well as decision making and problem solving/analytical thinking. Again, what is actually being assessed should be explicit. If it's not, it's OK to ask.

Group exercises are used when a lot of candidates are being assessed at the same time – perhaps as part of a graduate intake campaign or for sales or junior/middle managerial positions. You'll be working, not with actors this time, but with the other candidates who have got through the shortlisting process. Typically, there will be between four and six of you, and you'll be assigned a task to perform within a particular timeframe. This task could be practical and involve building something as a group using some props provided, or it could be more discussion-based and involve the group having to reach a consensus and decisions/recommendations on a particular issue.

Usually, no leader is appointed (although sometimes roles are assigned for the members of each group) and all candidates are given the same brief. Some exercises allow a certain amount of individual preparation time before the group gets together, and this will be made clear in the brief.

It's easy to assume that, because you're working with your competitors, you're being compared to them and rated against them. This is not the case. There will be assessors around the room observing the action or discussion and they'll be assigned one or two candidates to observe. You're therefore being assessed against the pre-determined criteria, not against each other.

Useful tips

Here are some tips for performing well in group exercises:

- As in role-play exercises, remember that it's mainly your style, rather than content, which is being assessed. It's very easy to forget this in the exercise itself, and observers often comment that within ten minutes, facades drop and real personalities start to emerge. It's best to be natural from the start!

- Often the best tactic is to position yourself, not necessarily as the group leader, but more as the group facilitator. This means helping the group to solve the issue by concentrating on the process. Try to be one of the first to speak and ask questions like: 'How do you think we should solve this task?' and 'Do we need to think about specific roles within the team?'

- Remember your interpersonal skills: smile, nod appreciatively, engage with all the others and ask questions. The observers will be looking for this.

- Deal with any disagreement or conflict by acknowledging the different ideas and inviting the individual concerned to say a bit more, and then invite opinions from around the group. Be prepared to back down politely. Showing yourself capable of being convinced shows flexibility, not weakness. If you strongly disagree, state your reasons clearly and invite further opinion.

In-basket or analysis exercises

There are a variety of written and scheduling exercises available for assessment centre use. The main difference between these and the role-play and group exercises we have discussed is that the emphasis is turned towards the actual content, as opposed to the way you deal with a person or group. As such, they are designed to measure the 'task' competencies we mentioned in Step 3, such as planning and organising, decision making or analytical thinking, as well as more generic 'written communication'.

In-basket exercises

In-basket exercises present you with a large pile of papers that may comprise email or letter correspondence, internal memos, requests for information and notes on telephone calls, for example. These papers are designed to reflect the typical tasks required of the job, particularly secretarial and administrative posts, and management roles. Your task is to sort these papers into some sort of meaningful order, determining priorities and identifying what actions would need to be taken.

These exercises look very complex, but there is not one 'ideal' solution. Instead, the assessors will be looking for the items you have prioritised, the actions you have suggested be taken and the way you multi-tasked and structured the exercise itself in the allotted time. These exercises will usually be measuring some element of planning and organising ability, as this can be measured both by your responses and actions and in the way you dealt with the time pressure of the exercise. They can last anything from an hour to three hours for the most complex ones.

Analysis exercises

Analysis or written exercises ask you to review a sizeable amount of written and numerical information through a variety of documents and then typically to write a report, analysing the information, summarising the key points and coming up with clear recommendations. The scenario is often one where you have to make recommendations on developing a new product or market, on implementing a new policy or on reviewing independent consultants' advice. The competencies being measured will often be similar to the ones mentioned on the previous page. Sometimes, there will be a linked presentation component to the exercise, where you have some time to prepare a presentation and present your findings to an imaginary board (made up of assessors). We will look at presentation exercises next.

Useful tips

Here are some tips for performing well in in-basket and analysis exercises:

■ Make sure you read the instructions carefully. What exactly are you being asked to do? For example, if the exercise scenario needs you to make contact with someone, are you being asked to determine who you would contact and in what order, or are you actually being asked to write the letter or email itself?

■ Stay calm and keep your eye on the time. There will be time to complete the task in the allotted time, so make a plan first and break the task up into parts – and time your completion of the parts along the way to ensure you're on track.

■ Remember that there's more than one way to prioritise items and perform tasks. Make it clear why you've tackled tasks in the way that you have.

Presentations

Some assessment exercises, such as the analysis or written ones described in the last section, incorporate a presentation as an add-on activity. Alternatively, you may be asked in advance of an assessment centre or as part of the interview process to prepare a presentation on PowerPoint (or similar) and to bring it with you to present on the day. Occasionally, you may be given half an hour on the day itself to prepare a presentation and deliver it there and then. The basic principles of presenting remain the same, and in-depth coverage of this form of assessment is given in a separate book in this series (*Presentation Skills in 7 Simple Steps*).

If selection processes include just one other assessment (apart from the interview), then it's usually either some form of psychometric testing or a presentation. The more senior the role, the more likely it is that a presentation will be asked for. Companies want to know whether someone can present their ideas in a persuasive, structured and clear way to an audience. Presentations therefore are usually measuring a combination of task competencies (decision making, analytical thinking, planning and organising, for example) and people competencies (such as communication skills, influencing and persuading).

You usually give your presentation at the beginning of an interview, and to the interview panel itself. Any questions they ask about the presentation (there is often a question and answer session afterwards) will lead on to the interview itself.

If the presentation is given as part of a wider assessment process, then it will be assessed in the same way as all the other assessments given, i.e. using competencies and marked by assessors. If it forms part of the interview, then in best-practice cases this will still happen; there will be a thorough, competency-based assessment of it, using trained assessors. Often, however, the interview panel will listen to it with a greater or lesser degree of objectivity! If there are no clear competencies being measured, the panel will be asking themselves more general questions such as:

- Is this person convincing?

- Does this person come across as credible?

- How would the staff respond if they were listening to this?

- Could I work with this person?

- Can I understand what they're saying?

The content of your presentation

The topic of your presentation could be literally anything. Most presentations will be work focused and related to the company or the job itself. For example, if you're applying for a purchasing role, you could be asked to present on a topic like: 'How would you ensure a good working relationship with our suppliers?'

Useful tips

Whatever the topic, take note of these tips for giving good presentations:

■ If you're using PowerPoint, keep the number of slides to a minimum: between five and eight for a ten-minute presentation. Don't clutter your slides, and try to use good quality pictures or graphics rather than lots of text or clip art.

■ Remember this adage: 'Tell them what you are going to tell them, then tell them, then tell them what you have told them!' This means giving an introduction before launching into your main topic, and finishing with a summary or conclusion.

■ Make sure that there is a logical flow to your presentation. The key points you make should take your listeners through a coherent story, with each element linked to the next.

■ Include content that appeals to the head (logic, facts, data) and heart (the impact on people of what you're saying, and the way you're saying it).

■ Use cue cards or memory prompts, but don't read from a script. This will enable you to concentrate on your body language and your voice. Stand up, speak slowly and clearly, use pausing and emphasis, and watch your audience.

■ Don't forget to keep your presentation to the time you have been allotted. Make sure you have practised it and noted timing milestones along the way.

Presenting yourself

Finally, it's worth taking some time to think in a bit more depth about how you present yourself. It's all too easy to lose yourself in the content of your presentation, whether on PowerPoint, flipchart paper or other props, and forget about preparing yourself.

■ First, refer back to the advice on dealing with interview nerves in Step 5. Arrive in plenty of time, stop those negative thoughts, focus on your strengths and keep a sense of perspective.

■ Second, practise, practise, and then practise some more. Start by giving the presentation to yourself in a mirror, then ask a friend to watch you, time you and give you feedback. This will not only help you learn your material, but will ensure it's well-timed and will increase your confidence – thereby reducing nerves.

■ Third, watch your body language. Stand up if the room allows it, keep your shoulders back and imagine a string pulling you up from the top of your head. Make sure your hands are out of your pockets and use them to emphasise points. Use plenty of eye contact (look at the whole panel, not just the ones who appear interested) and smile.

■ Finally, don't forget your voice. Speak clearly and slowly (especially if you have an accent) and try to avoid fillers such as 'um' and 'er'. Project your voice and notice whether your audience is following you. If not, pause, and ask if everything is clear.

Dealing with assessment centres

A selection process may use none, one or all of these types of assessment. As we've mentioned, when a number of these are put together into a one- or sometimes two-day process, this is known as an assessment centre. They are a very thorough (if expensive) way of determining whether the person is right for the job. If you get invited to one, you can congratulate yourself that you've probably got through a thorough sifting process and will be one of the five or six candidates deemed to be worth looking at closely.

You can give yourself the best chance for performing as well as you are able (which, as we have mentioned, is what the assessments are designed to achieve as well) by making sure you do the following:

- Practise your presentation, rehearse your interview responses and remember your strengths.

- Get a good night's sleep the night before and have a substantial breakfast to keep your energy levels up.

- Ensure you give yourself plenty of time for the journey and plan it in advance.

- Be aware that the assessors will be around the whole time. While they should not be formally assessing you outside the specific exercises, be professional at all times.

- Treat every exercise as a fresh start and a new opportunity to demonstrate your skills and strengths.

- If you can, keep your mobile phone off at all times and particularly during exercises.

After the assessments

When all the assessments are complete, you'll be thanked and asked to leave. The day is not over for the assessors, however. Several hours usually follow where they take each candidate in turn and review the scores given for each competency and each exercise. The emphasis will be on a fair and objective assessment, rather than simply comparing candidates against each other. Only at the very end of the process do the candidates get compared with each other in terms of the scores they achieved, to enable the assessors to make selection decisions.

Remember that if you performed well, you may be considered 'also suitable' if you don't get offered the job this time round – and you never know what opportunities might occur as a result.

Receiving feedback

Whatever form of assessment you've undertaken – even if it's just an interview – it's ethical selection practice to offer all candidates feedback on their performance. This is essential for your own learning and development, and taking feedback on board and changing what needs to be changed will help you achieve success next time round. If you're not offered feedback, then ask for it – even if you're offered the job!

When receiving feedback by phone, letter or email, try not to get defensive but just listen or read as dispassionately as you can. Treat it as data: information you can do something with to make you better next time. Try not to make excuses (and definitely not in conversation with the giver of the feedback) but treat it as a gift to help your future. If the feedback is vague, ask for some specific examples to help you improve next time. Ensure that you thank them for taking the time – either in person or by email if you can – and tell them how useful you have found the process.

If you're upset by the feedback, the important thing is to keep a sense of perspective. By going through the process, and learning from the feedback, you're in a great position to do better next time!

Key take-aways

Think about the things you will take away from Step 6 and how you will implement them.

Topic	Take-away	Implementation
Understanding the importance of assessments and why companies use them	• *An assessment centre is a range of assessments put together in one event to test multiple candidates at the same time.* • *They assess evidence of me performing the competency.*	• *Expect my application process to include at least one form of assessment.* • *Prepare by understanding the types of assessment typically used.*
What to expect during, and how to perform well in, psychometric tests		
What to expect during, and how to perform well in, role-plays		
What to expect during, and how to perform well in, group exercises		
What to expect during, and how to perform well in, analysis/written exercises		
What to expect during, and how to give, presentations		
Dealing with assessment centres		
Receiving feedback		

Step 7

SURVIVE AND THRIVE IN YOUR NEW JOB

'Work is much more fun than fun.' — Sir Noël Coward (1899–1973), playwright and actor

Five ways to succeed

- Get feedback whatever the result of your application.
- Be prepared to negotiate salary and benefits.
- Be professional during your notice period.
- Find a mentor.
- Manage your new boss!

Five ways to fail

- Don't think about your minimum salary expectations.
- Tell your old boss what you think of them.
- Don't ask for support from your new colleagues.
- Don't attend your new company induction.
- Pay no attention to what your new boss wants.

Dealing with rejection and acceptance

There are three possible outcomes from your job application:

■ **Rejection**

The first is that you get a rejection letter or email (or more rarely, a phone call). The important thing here is to keep a sense of perspective. Allow yourself to be hurt for a while – chat it through with a friend – but try not to take it personally. After all, it merely means that on the day, someone else was chosen over you, but that doesn't mean you have failed. You've gained valuable experience, you've done a lot of preparatory work for the next time round and, if you've followed the processes in this book you gave yourself every possible chance.

Even though you may not feel like it right now, ensure that you're given feedback on your whole application – the application itself, your interview and any assessments you were asked to complete. If this isn't offered, you should ask for it – it will demonstrate that you've got resilience and a desire to learn from the process. Handle the situation with politeness and dignity at all times – there may be another vacancy at that particular organisation you may want to apply for.

■ **'Also suitable'**

The second outcome is that you don't get offered the job, but you are classed as an 'also suitable'. The organisation may ask if they can keep your record on file – or they may even ask you to apply for a different role. If this happens, you can congratulate yourself on doing a thorough job and decide whether or not the new role is something you want. Organisations rarely do this unless they're serious about potentially employing you in the future, so it's important to see past the 'almost but not quite' feeling of disappointment you may feel.

Any initial emotions about failure will soon fade and you'll then be able to think logically about the alternatives on offer and future opportunities. You've done the hard bit – successfully selling your skills and strengths to an organisation that knew nothing about you at the start of the process. Keep an open mind – you don't know what might result from this. It may even take your career in a new and exciting direction that you previously hadn't considered!

■ **You get the job!**

The third outcome is that you are offered the job. This is likely to be a euphoric moment initially, but one that's usually followed by anxiety as you review the implications – often in the first few seconds! This is completely normal, so don't worry. Take a deep breath and, if you've received the offer by telephone, on no account simply accept … you want to make sure you find out what's on offer and get the right deal.

Getting the right deal

There's a saying in negotiation that the first person to mention a figure is the one that loses out. This is the time to play it cool, calm and collected. If the organisation has gone through a recruitment process and has decided it wants you at the end of it, then you have more power than you might imagine. They've invested money in the process of finding the right person, so until you formally accept, in many ways you're in the driving seat.

Of course, this doesn't mean you should sound as if you're doing them a favour! You want to give the impression that you're very interested in the position and would like to know a bit more about what's being offered in terms of salary and other benefits.

Don't forget that often the only time you get to negotiate your salary is when you're accepting the job. It's much harder once you're working somewhere to subsequently ask for a pay rise, so make the most of this unique opportunity. The other thing to remember is that it's not just about the money. Companies often have little leeway on the advertised salary but may have more flexibility on associated benefits.

So, when asking about what's on offer, consider the following:

■ **Basic salary**

It's rare to get in excess of ten per cent above the advertised or previously discussed figure, so unless you have other job offers in the pipeline, aim for a sensible compromise. Get them to come up with a figure first and, if you're less than happy with it, ask if a rise could be built in once a satisfactory probation period has been reached.

■ **Bonuses**

Does the job have a bonus element? If so, is it an individual one or a team one – or in some cases, based on the whole organisation's performance? If so, ask how many times this has been paid over the last few years.

■ **Pension**

This will usually be the standard organisational offering, but it can make a huge difference to the overall package, so it's worth finding out what is being offered.

■ **Holiday entitlement**

Find out the company rules regarding length of service (some entitlements go up the longer you work there) and whether a certain number of days can be carried over. Some companies have schemes that enable you to buy or sell holiday entitlement.

■ **Training and development**

Ask if you'll have a defined allowance and what opportunities are available.

■ **Other possibilities**

Ask about medical insurance, relocation support, if necessary, and season ticket loans for commuting purposes.

The negotiation

Once you're clear about what's being offered, thank them very much, let them know that you're still interested in the position and ask for some time (usually overnight but no more than a couple of days, if possible) to think about their offer. They'll be expecting you to negotiate, but also to be reasonable.

When it comes to the actual negotiation, do this in person if you can, but bear in mind that this negotiation is usually conducted over the phone. Many people feel embarrassed when talking about money, but try to put this feeling to one side and be calm, reasonable and clear about your expectations. If the offer is very low, politely express your disappointment and ask how flexible they can be with this or other compensating benefits. Don't talk about your personal circumstances (they're irrelevant), instead focus on what you can offer the organisation and what you think you're worth to them.

Here are some pointers to help you negotiate your way to the best possible outcome:

■ Aim for win/win

Keep in mind that a successful negotiation is one where both parties feel that they've got a satisfactory outcome. This means you should listen to their point of view, consider their needs and be prepared to compromise to some extent. You should also be professional, good humoured and non-confrontational throughout. Remember that if you're successful you'll end up working with them!

■ Have a clear idea of your walk-away point

What's the minimum acceptable figure, below which you would be prepared to walk away from the offer? Keep this figure in mind at all times. If you take the time to prepare here, you'll feel – and sound – more confident.

■ Be as flexible as you can

Don't forget that you'll need to consider the whole package on offer – don't just focus on the actual salary but also the associated benefits. Think in terms of the whole deal.

■ Remind them why they should employ you

If they appear hesitant or don't seem to be moving from their initial position, try to address any specific concerns they may have and reiterate the value that you feel you would add to their organisation. Don't forget that they've offered you the job, so they must feel this too. Be firm and clear – and remember the three points above.

More in-depth coverage of how to negotiate successfully can be found in a separate book in this series (*Negotiation Skills in 7 Simple Steps*).

Saying yes – or no!

If you feel, after all the negotiations appear to be over, that the rewards being offered are simply not enough, you always have the option of rejecting the offer. You should have your 'walk-away figure' in mind and if it appears that they're not willing to meet you, then it's perfectly acceptable to say no. It's a hard decision to make, but you never know – saying a final 'no' may get them to reconsider. Be polite, thank them again for their time and say that, with regret, you will decline their kind offer and hope that they find a suitable candidate. On no account use this as a bluff, however. If you say no, you must be absolutely prepared to walk away.

If you are walking away, then, it's important to do it in the right way. You need to leave them with the impression that you were calm, clear-headed, independent-minded and, above all, gracious – and maybe a little disappointed yet philosophical. Leaving them this way means that you have a greater chance of ending up working for them at some point in the future.

If you end up getting a deal that you're happy with, then thank them for their flexibility and let them know that if they were to confirm those terms in writing, you would be delighted to accept. This is now the time to ask about start dates and whether there's anything they would like you to do in the meantime (for example, you might be asked to go in and meet the team for lunch one day in advance of the start date).

Finally, make sure you contact those people who will be providing references for you to warn them to expect contact from the company or organisation concerned.

Leaving your old job

Unless this is your first job or you've spent some time in training or unemployed, you now have to leave your old job. Here, you should be aiming for a dignified exit that makes all parties look good and makes the best out of what is sometimes a difficult situation.

I've seen many examples of how not to do this over the years. Perhaps one of the worst was someone who thought this would be a perfect opportunity to tell her boss exactly what she thought of her, forgetting of course, that her boss was one of the people she'd asked to write a reference for her. The phrase 'Never burn your bridges behind you' is one to remember here – not only may references be involved, but very often people go back to work where they once did years before. It's always to everyone's advantage to leave on a positive and constructive note. Simply say that it's time for you to move on and that you've been given an opportunity that you didn't want to turn down, while mentioning that there have been many good aspects to working in your current organisation and that you're grateful for the development it has given you.

The principle here, then, is the same as the way we turn down an unacceptable offer, discussed on the previous page. You want to leave with everyone having a favourable impression of you because you never know whether you might end up working there again – or whether your old boss will join your new company!

Notice periods

It's usual for longer notice periods (three months or so) to be negotiated down, although this does depend on the job itself. Most notice periods are a lot shorter than this – say a month – and it may still be worth your while to negotiate it down to a couple of weeks, if you can, to give yourself a break before the new job starts in earnest.

It's difficult not to feel a bit in limbo during this period, but again, the key point here is to make sure you leave in as positive a way as possible. Don't worry if, during this period, you get pangs of regret or start questioning your wisdom in leaving. This is entirely normal and just a part of the leaving cycle. Acknowledge that there will be sad parts as well as the excitement of the new, and try to keep a sense of perspective.

It may be harder to leave positively if the reason for your leaving is through redundancy or being sacked. If this is the case, try to separate out your feelings (which are likely to be of hurt, anger and betrayal) from your behaviour. If you can go through this while still appearing upbeat and professional, it will reflect very well on you.

Keep at the back of your mind that you're moving on to bigger and better things and, if your current job has not worked out for specific reasons, then you now have an opportunity to learn from this and make sure, as much as you can, that it doesn't happen again. Also remember that there's no stigma whatsoever in being made redundant; it has happened to more people than you might realise.

Exit interviews

You may well be asked to go through an exit interview. This is good practice on behalf of the employer. Exit interviews help an organisation to learn about its systems and processes, its culture and working environment.

This is a good opportunity to be honest, to say what has led you to leave and to give your opinions on how things could change. Again, don't burn any bridges here – be positive and constructive in any criticism you make, giving options for improvement if you can. And don't forget to say what you feel is good about the place too! Aim to make them feel you're parting as friends as much as possible.

Usually, such interviews are performed by an HR professional, although sometimes your manager may conduct it instead. More often than not, it will consist of a number of set questions asking for your reasons for leaving and helping them to address any issues that may have led to your leaving. Typical questions include:

- ■ What is your main reason for leaving?

- ■ How do you feel about the organisation?

- ■ How would you describe the culture of this organisation?

- ■ How could the organisation have made the best use of your skills?

- ■ What has been difficult or frustrating in your time with us?

- ■ What could we have done to prevent this happening?

- ■ What other advice would you give us?

And even:

- ■ Could you be persuaded to discuss the possibility of staying?

Try to keep in mind that many organisations genuinely want to know why you're leaving and how they can prevent experienced people leaving in the future. If you're constructive in your criticism and clear about what the organisation does well and what you've got personally from your time with them, it will work in your favour should you ever want to return.

Starting your new job

This is the exciting – and scary – part!

Surviving the first day

It would be unusual if you weren't a little nervous or apprehensive about going in for your first day in a new job. Remember that as long as they don't go into overdrive, nerves are a good thing as they help us to remain sharp and focused. If you feel overly nervous, however, then use the techniques for dealing with nerves discussed in Step 5.

If you think it will help, do a practice run of your route to work, at the time you would normally be travelling, so you can see what it's like; the first day won't feel quite so unknown then. Some people find it helps their stress levels to arrive half an hour early on the first day and gather their thoughts and mentally prepare themselves with a coffee nearby.

Follow the same rules as we mentioned in Step 5 with regard to dress. Unless you specifically know differently, it's better to overdress and see what other people are wearing rather than be the only one in shorts and flip flops!

Inductions

Most organisations will have some form of induction plan for you. This will sometimes be a whole-organisation welcome event, and/or a specific departmental or team induction. Inductions should go beyond telling you what day of the month you'll be paid, what the company's equality and diversity policy is and how to work safely, important as all these things may be. They should include tours around the building or buildings to help you acclimatise.

Perhaps more importantly, you should be able to get a feel for how your particular part of the organisation fits into the whole and how your job fits in with the departmental goals. New employees quite often leave in the first few months if they haven't been helped to adjust to the culture of the particular organisation.

Your manager should help you understand the departmental structure, the key requirements of the job and how your probationary period and ongoing appraisal system will operate. They will usually be assisted by HR, health and safety officers, a representative from the learning and development team, and possibly company representatives from trades unions and sports and social clubs. If you don't get offered any of this, a polite request to your new manager will usually work if you're specific about what information will help you.

Sometimes, you may be assigned a mentor or 'buddy': this can be one of the most useful initiatives to help speed up the settling-in period. If one is provided for you, all well and good, but if not, it may be a good idea to find one yourself.

Managing your new boss

The relationship you have with your manager has one of the biggest impacts on whether you enjoy – and stay in – your job. There's a saying: 'Most people leave the boss, not the job.' I spend most of my life training managers to manage people better, and I've found this to be true. The way you start this relationship, then, is key to your enjoyment and success in the first few months.

Of course, there are bad bosses. But there are lots of good ones too, and most just want you to perform in the role you've been employed to do and to help you to do it to the best of your ability. If you feel confident enough, it's a good idea to ask your new boss upfront: 'How do you want us to work together?' This can be a very helpful way of starting the relationship. Perhaps the critical thing is to find out what your manager wants from you, and there's no shortcut to finding out the answer – you need to have this conversation with them.

Your relationship with your manager will change, too. As you both get to know each other's working style, strengths and weaknesses, you may have to re-evaluate the relationship from time to time. What is essential now, however, is that you start on the right footing. Good communication is key here.

As soon as you start your new job, get clarity from your manager on these key questions:

- ■ What do you see as my key objectives for the first three months?

- ■ How will we know whether I'm succeeding?

- ■ How would you like me to report back to you? And how often?

- ■ What are my first priorities? What can stop me achieving these?

- ■ What support can I expect?

- ■ What feedback should I expect?

After a month or so, ask for feedback and try to arrange monthly one-to-one meetings if you can. Ask what your manager thinks you've done well, and what they'd like you to be doing differently. Respond positively to their feedback, to encourage them to give you more. Building this relationship in the early stages of your job will repay the time spent many times over – and will make your new job more rewarding, too.

Mentoring

Having a mentor can be one of the most important and enriching developmental relationships you will ever have, and it can really smooth your passage into a new role or organisation. Most of us have experienced having a mentor at some point in our lives. We probably didn't call it mentoring, of course. It may have been a sports club leader when we were teenagers, or a member of a voluntary group. It may even have been an older brother or sister.

Mentoring can be a powerful experience in a variety of circumstances and settings. You may have a professional mentor, someone who steers and guides you through your chosen profession. If you're studying to be an accountant or mechanic or undertaking an apprenticeship, for example, you may be assigned a mentor or supervisor who will help you to log your experience and give you professional and career guidance.

If this isn't your first job, think back to when you joined your last organisation. What would have helped you in your first few months? What would help you now to get to know how the organisation really works? We don't always want to take these sorts of questions to our managers.

This last point is one of the major benefits to you in finding an organisational mentor. No matter how supportive your manager is, it may not always feel 'safe' to ask awkward questions or explore future career development or concerns about operational issues. Mentoring can provide a safe forum to ask these questions or simply to explore concerns or future opportunities.

In addition, it's time out of the stresses of the job for the mentee as well as the mentor. Don't underestimate the power of this space to think. It can really help in putting things into perspective, especially if you add the value of having an independent 'mirror' to bounce ideas off. A good mentor is motivational and inspiring too. You can learn from their successes and mistakes, and get their advice on what works best. Mentees often report after a mentoring session that they feel enthused, energised and ready to face the job with renewed vigour!

If you don't get assigned a mentor or 'buddy', then ask your new manager if they could suggest someone. It should be someone impartial (so not in your immediate team) and someone who has been in the organisation for a while. Make it known why you would find it useful to have someone to help guide you in this new phase of your working life and to help you shape your ideas. Think in advance about what you want from such a relationship. To get the most out of a mentoring relationship, follow these basic guidelines:

■ Prepare for each meeting with your mentor so that you're clear about what you want to achieve in it.

■ Be open to feedback and challenge, and ultimately be open to change.

■ Value the insights of the mentor, but not necessarily as the only way forward. Your own views and experiences are equally valid, so just add your mentor's to the mix!

■ Be open, honest and reliable in all interactions and agree to basic levels of confidentiality.

And finally ...

You deserve a pat on the back. Take the time to really celebrate your success. If you've followed the steps in this book you'll have put yourself in the best position possible not only to get that job, but also to make the most of it once you're there. Success often builds on success and if you keep on reviewing your skills and strengths, noticing when you're at your most motivated and whether you're performing in accordance with your true values, then you'll make it more likely that this job will be followed by a better one, if that's what you want.

We've mentioned many times in this book that being proactive – taking the initiative by first understanding what you really want, working out the steps to get there and keeping this under constant review – will get you the career you deserve. Respond to feedback and try to have the attitude that constant learning and development help both you and the organisation you choose to work for. Keep on developing yourself, develop and stretch the role you're in, and you never know what will be possible.

I wish you the very best of luck and success in getting that job!

Key take-aways

Think about the things you will take away from Step 7 and how you will implement them.

Topic	Take-away	Implementation
Dealing with rejection and acceptance	• *Don't take rejection personally.* • *Don't forget – I may be an 'also suitable'.* • *If offered a position, don't accept the first offer.*	• *Ask for feedback if it's not automatically offered.* • *Learn from the whole process by thoroughly reviewing each step.* • *Be prepared to negotiate!*
Making sure you get the right deal		
Leaving your old job		
Surviving the first day of your new job		
Managing your new boss		
Finding a mentor		